ARCHITECTURAL
TERRA COTTA
of
GLADDING, McBEAN

Entrance Cartouche, Weinstock-Lubin Building, Sacramento, 1924

Ernest Molinario, far right, and other sculptors pose for a self-portrait in 1922. Molinario has draped the cable release over his foot. Next to him sits Vittorio Russo. P. O. Tognelli sits with his arm around his son Willie. In the back row, from left to right, is F. Allamand, Squalla, J. W. Nickerson, and young Ernest Kadel holding a cigar.

PHOTOGRAPHY NOTES

The "spirit of place" is felt by everyone who walks into the modeling room of the Gladding, McBean pottery. The excitement of discovery and the desire to share this *genius loci* has motivated me to photograph the Lincoln plant over a ten-year period. Inside the huge wood-frame building housing the modeling room, light streams through clearstories and tall windows along the walls, illuminating both objects and space. The vast room is like an interior landscape in constant flux as sunlight moves through it. Artifacts of the past and present resonate with nostalgia and humor. Immediately upon entering, one senses the magic, almost spiritual quality imparted by the dramatic lighting, the thin coating of fine clay dust that permeates everything, and the phantasmagoria of architectural relics.

For a photographer, the interiors of the Gladding, McBean pottery are both a challenge and a delight. I first visited the plant in January 1981, with photographer Nikki Pahl. We were led through the fascinating and historic buildings, through the searing heat of the kiln rooms, the cool moistness of the molding rooms and the incredible array of artifacts in the modeling room. I was struck by the dramatic natural lighting and the variety of visual images that were everywhere. Our "tour" ended at a small closet off the modeling room. Here were stored thousands of photographic negatives documenting many decades of architectural terra cotta history. We were stunned not only with the number of negatives, but by their striking quality.

Photography has a short history compared to other art forms. To a contemporary photographer, finding a cache of seventy and eighty-year-old negatives is like an archeologist's discovery of a thousand-year-old treasure vault: it is an unforgettable experience. I made two resolutions: the first was to return to photograph the plant; and second, to preserve and print the historic photographic collection.

On subsequent trips to the Lincoln pottery I began making the photographs that appear in this book. The kiln room was the most challenging to photograph. Armed with an 8 × 10″ camera, I tried to capture the vibrating contrasts of light and dark in the long avenue of massive bee-hive kilns, where bright shafts of light cut through the dark, hot atmosphere.

I have found the multi-layers of time an intriguing subject. A vigorous clay modeler of 1989 works in surroundings which have evolved from the late 19th century. Many of the details surrounding him are the same as those of 1900. This is the case not because of a lack of modernization, but because the method of producing hand-made terra cotta is essentially unchanged over the years. The plant has remained intact. In an era when so many historical factories are being torn down, this is a refreshing phenomenon.

In 1985 I suggested to David Lucchetti, president of Pacific Coast Building Products, now the parent company of Gladding, McBean that we find a safer place to store the collection. We arranged with Gary Kurutz, head of Special Collections at the California State Library, to move the collection to the library. Mr. Kurutz's keen interest in California photography and history and his enthusiasm in building a fine collection at the State Library made him uniquely suited as custodian for this valuable photographic archive.

Meanwhile, Mr. Lucchetti agreed that Pacific Coast Building Products would fund a preservation project for the negatives. Bill Wyatt, the pottery's official historian and his wife Doris, joined me for a three-month marathon of cleaning and filing. We started with the oldest negatives, the 8 × 10″ glass plates, then on to the fragile nitrate negatives, and finally to the more recent safety film-base negatives, until at last, one-hundred years of photography was revealed. The carefully packed collection was then trucked to the California State Library in Sacramento.

From the meticulous job records kept by Gladding, McBean and from retired plant workers we have learned a great deal about the use of the camera in the production of architectural terra cotta. The 8 × 10″ view camera was introduced around 1890 to make the job of communication between the plant and architects easier. Since there was no official "photographer" at the pottery, one or another of the predominantly Italian craftsmen was pressed into service. His assignment was not to make "artistic" photographs of the terra cotta work, but to show each clay piece to best advantage; the backgrounds were extraneous. The piece was arranged so that minute surface details were well-lighted and a ruler was placed at the foot of the piece to indicate scale. Some of the early photos had the backgrounds painted out, leaving the sculpted object in silhouette. The camera lens was a little wider than normal and an f.64 stop was used, which demanded a long exposure in the natural interior light of the modeling room. The camera proved successful in conveying the modelers' work to Gladding, McBean's widely scattered clients. When a clay model was particularly impressive, like the Spreckels shield or the Fireman's Fund capital, the artists would arrange themselves with pride around their art work to be photographed. The camera was also used to create studies to assist the

sculptors. Plant employees or members of their families were posed to represent Roman gods and goddesses, cherubs or satyrs. The photos were then used to check anatomical proportions of the works-in-progress.

Each photograph of a modeled piece also included the job number for easy identification. For a major project there might be hundreds of photographic details required, and clear identification was essential. Prints were then made and sent to the architect, who would indicate approval by signing the reverse side. When the photograph was returned the company would stamp it with the date received. After the terra cotta piece was finished and shipped, the photograph of the model was kept in the client file for reference in case the piece was broken in transit or during installation and had to be remade.

The darkroom was one of those after-thoughts added into the modeling room space. In this surprisingly cramped and poorly ventilated six-by-six foot room, glass, and later film negatives were developed and printed. Temperatures in the Sacramento Valley range from a high of 115 degrees to well below 40 degrees fahrenheit. Imagine working in total darkness on a hot valley day, developing glass negatives in a toxic solution of Pyro Gallic. The fumes, heat and poor ventilation must have been unbearable, if not dangerous. The consistency of one's negatives would have been a constant problem. When I printed negatives from the collection, I found a range of from 0 to 5 filter grades. Thus, I could guess if the negatives had been developed in summer or winter.

Some of the early work was printed on cyanotype paper, rendering delicate blue images that still exist. I found invoices for gold chloride, evidence of "printing out" (studio paper) being used: this would have been a choice paper for the denser negatives. Many images were printed on matte paper so that when they were submitted to the architect he could sketch over the model in pencil. Watercolors were used to illustrate how a polychrome piece would appear.

Around 1900, Ernest Molinario became the *de facto* photographer at the Lincoln plant. As we know today, Molinario's most memorable accomplishments at Gladding, McBean were his photographs. Many of the best photos of the historic collection are his.

In 1924 Ernest Cardini and Carlos Tagliabue, expert sculptors, were hired in Italy by Peter McBean. In Lincoln, Cardini took responsibility of the photography until he left during World War II. Ray Johnson, now chief of drafting for Gladding, McBean, was the last "photographer" to use the 8 × 10″ camera. After Interpace bought the company in 1962, the venerable old camera disappeared. The photographic record left by these non-professional cameramen is testimony to their skill as artisans. Like their work in terra cotta, which still adorns many buildings in California and elsewhere, their photographs are worthy of preservation.

Mary Swisher, 1989

ACKNOWLEDGMENTS

The author wishes to express deep gratitude to all those who aided in making possible the creation of this book, K. D. Kurutz, author of an early article on Gladding, McBean and photographer Mary Swisher who patiently read the manuscript and made numerous useful suggestions. Kathy Kurutz assisted by tracking down vital information in Los Angeles. Mead B. Kibbey, a photographic historian and patron of remarkable talent, provided encouragement, advice and "opened doors" at critical times. Publishers Linda and Wayne Bonnett, through the happy circumstances of a visit to the State Library, quickly recognized the potential of the images and the Gladding, McBean story and provided their considerable talents in sculpting this pictorial history. Susan Tunick's knowledge, enthusiasm, guidance and inspiration throughout this project proved essential.

Without the assistance of the dedicated and enthusiastic employees of Gladding, McBean this work would not have been possible. Fred Anderson and David Lucchetti of Pacific Coast Building Products generously donated to the State Library the Gladding McBean Photograph collection. Company historian Bill Wyatt gave freely of his time and graciously shared his considerable knowledge of the company's past. Plant Superintendent Gene Watt opened doors and files, Ray Johnson of the Drafting Room made available rare periodicals and technical information, and nurse Virginia Bess permitted use of her space and equipment and rescued Mary and me from the cold of the Lincoln winter.

The staff of the California State Library has been most supportive and patient during this endeavor. Appreciation is extended to State Librarian Gary E. Strong for computerizing the Lincoln job order book and Rick Reyes for the data entry. Sheila Thornton, Chief of State Library Services, offered support and release time for needed trips to Lincoln. In the Library's California Section, Richard Terry, Vickie Lockhardt, Kathy Eustis, Sibylle Zemitis and Shirley MacKay were enormously helpful as were Tere Silva, Donna Emerson and Rick Rae of the Preservation Office.

William Strum of the Oakland History Room of the Oakland Public Library, Barbara Lekisch of the California Historical Society Library, architectural historian Karen Weitze, Michael Several of Los Angeles, Lucinda Woodward of the California State Office of Historic Preservation, Waverly Lowell of the Friends of Terra Cotta, and Joseph A. Taylor of the Tile Heritage Foundation all provided aid or suggestions.

Gary F. Kurutz 1989

My deepest appreciation goes to Bill Wyatt who has given generously of his knowledge and time for the past ten year. Nikki Pahl, who has worked with me on the historical negative collection through her pregnancy and motherhood has a special place in my "hall of gratitude." Robert Swisher gave me valuable advice while Anika and Elizabeth Swisher were excellent darkroom assistants . . . they all have my love and gratitude.

In addition, I'm indebted to K. D. Kurutz for her early interest in showing my photographs at the Crocker Art Museum and Susan Tunick who arranged a showing of my work in New York. Michael Stratton, from Ironbridge, England has my accolade for his persistent spirit as an industrial archeologist.

Individual thanks go to Kendall LeCompte who listened, advised, and accompanied me to Oakland, to Jo Mills at Lightwork, Vickie Lockhardt Rose Yoshii, and Terri Silva at the California State Library. My appreciation goes to Trudy Cook of the Los Angeles Athletic Club who gave Gary and me an informative welcome to downtown Los Angeles and to Takeshi Shukuya who drove me to an early morning "shoot." Mead Kibbey has been an incomparable mentor and Aaron Gallup has shared information on Sacramento architecture.

Doris and Bill Wyatt were my chief workers on the negative preservation project. Other volunteers were Don Postle, Nikki Pahl, Michaele LeCompte, Kendall LeCompte, Bill Dillinger, Elizabeth Swisher, and Marian Sharpe, who all have my gratitude.

Last but most importantly I wish to acknowledge the contribution of those at "The Pottery": Gene Watts has opened doors and answered endless questions; Ray Johnson and the drafting room, Pete Pederson, Mary Ensey, and Tom Sawyer of the architectural terra cotta department; Carolyn Adams and the office staff; Harry Tracy and the pressing department, Jesus Cardenas and the modeling and plaster department; Mel Gordon of Glazing; Normita Callison, Chemistry; Nathan Parra and the fitting department; Nello Stefani, carpentry; Fred Enos of maintenance; Sonny Price, superintendent of the kilns; and Virginia Bess who shared her office, copy machine, and warm heart. A thanks to Fred Anderson for his early interest in my work and to Dave Lucchetti who continued and nurtured that interest.

Finally I wish to dedicate my images to all the artisans both past and present whose spirit has inspired my photographs.

Mary Swisher 1989

HISTORIC PHOTOGRAPHS ACKNOWLEDGMENTS

All historic photographs are reproduced with the permission of the California State Library, Sacramento, California, with the following exceptions: Page 12, 37, courtesy Gabriel Moulin Studios, San Francisco; page 75, 77, 78, 80, 81, 84, 88, 104, 118, courtesy Gladding, McBean & Company, Lincoln, California.

729.5

Library of Congress Cataloging-in-Publication Data

```
Kurutz, Gary F.
    Architectural terra cotta of Gladding, McBean.

    Includes bibliographical references.
    1. Architectural terra-cotta--United States.
2. Decoration and ornament, Architectural--United States.
3. Facades--United States.  4. Architecture, Modern--19th
century--United States.  5. Architecture, Modern--20th
century--United States.  6. Gladding, McBean and Company.
I. Title.
NA3700.K87  1989          729'.5          89-25008
ISBN 0-915269-09-0
```

FIRST PRINTING   2-90   2200

Printed in Japan by Toppan Printing Co., Ltd., Tokyo
through Overseas Printing Corporation, San Francisco

Published by WINDGATE PRESS P.O. Box 1715, Sausalito, California 94966

Garland Theater, Los Angeles, 1912

C O N T E N T S

ARCHITECTURAL
TERRA COTTA
of
GLADDING, McBEAN

Gary F. Kurutz

Contemporary Photography
Mary Swisher

Introduction
Susan Tunick

WINDGATE PRESS: SAUSALITO, CALIFORNIA

INTRODUCTION

With the near demise of the terra cotta industry during the Great Depression of the 1930s, the majority of records, objects, and photographs disappeared, leaving barely a trace of the numerous companies which had grown and prospered across the country. Until the publication of *The Architectural Terra Cotta of Gladding, McBean,* the primary resource through which one could piece together the fascinating history of the American architectural terra cotta industry was *The Story of Terra Cotta,* published seventy years ago. According to the copyright page, it was "printed for subscribers only and is limited to one hundred copies," each of which was hand-numbered. Written by Walter Geer, president of one of the leading companies at the time, it offered a highly personal account of the subject. In it, Geer explored the development of the industry and provided salient information about the forty-eight companies that were active in the early 1900s.

As a counterpoint to this very broad approach, *The Architectural Terra Cotta of Gladding, McBean* offers the first and, most likely, the only in-depth study of a single major terra cotta company. The combination of two remarkable facts — that Gladding, McBean & Company has remained in operation since 1875 and that much of the company's early job documentation has been preserved in the California State Library — has served to make it possible for this insightful and perceptive work to be prepared.

Terra cotta brought new expressiveness to the architecture and skylines of cities across America. Since the 19th century, building facades and rooflines have been ornamented with terra cotta, either in its natural clay colors or glazed with matte or glossy finishes. Vivid yellows, greens, and cobalt blues as well as metallic lusters of silver and gold emphasized lavish architectural detailing. These vibrant colors marked a long period of extraordinary richness in building design. To the individual who appreciates abundant ornament, the architecture of recent decades has left a spare, even austere collection of buildings devoid of both color and detail. But there is still pleasure to be gained by seeking out the architectural styles of the late 19th and early 20th centuries. By looking beyond the severe, often banal lines of recent design, it is still possible to discover a gargoyle peering down from a neighboring building or to see an archway seemingly held aloft by winged cherubs. Above hastily modernized facades lies a vast and varied display of exotic imagery, color, and texture.

"This is an innovation. It is indestructible and as hard and as smooth as any porcelain ware. It will be washed by every rainstorm and may if necessary be scrubbed like a dinner plate."[1] These words were used in the 1894 *Economist* to describe Chicago's new Reliance Building designed by Daniel H. Burnham. Its smooth and indestructible surface that resembled porcelain ware was actually glossy-white glazed terra cotta cladding used to encase the steel-cage construction of the building. Although terra cotta was first used in America in the 1870s to ornament masonry structures which had load-bearing walls, the material also accommodated the strides made in building technology. In the 1880s, with the invention of the self-supporting metal frame, the elevator, and fireproof construction, tall buildings — first known as "cloud-scrapers" — began to

develop. Skyscrapers introduced a new concept, the "curtain-wall," a non-load-bearing enclosure for the metal skeletal structure. Terra cotta was an ideal material with which to clothe the building's skeleton. This new building method presented structural engineers with an innovation that would change buildings more than any other development since the flying buttress.

Terra cotta, literally "burnt earth," is a term that has been used loosely since Roman times to refer to a glazed or unglazed ceramic ware intended primarily for architectural elements and large statuary. The clay or clays from which terra cotta is made are carefully selected for specific properties. In many cases the clay body finally used is a mixture of different clays from widely scattered sources, all carefully measured and combined following exact formulas. A terra cotta clay body frequently includes sand or *grog* (pulverized pre-fired clay) to help reduce shrinkage and subsequent warpage during manufacture. Terra cotta can be coated with white, black, buff, or colored glazes. In ancient times, prior to the development of glazes in 15th century Italy, the color of terra cotta was a range of earth tones resulting from natural pigmentation present in the clay deposit. Thus, the earth's own coloring, such as iron oxide, added variety to the molded clay surface.

According to Walter Geer, terra cotta offered a far better reflection of the personality of the architect than any other building material. There was no other material which could be so readily impressed with the conception of the artist as "clay in the hand of the potter." Except for small decorative elements, architectural terra cotta was not stocked by material dealers. Rather, each job was individually executed with special attention paid to each set of structural conditions. "More so than any other architectural product, terra cotta is 'hand-tailored' to the finest degree — not simply the embodiment in three dimensions of a set of drawings, but the complete expression of the architectural idea in terms of a certain combination of colors, glazes, surface textures, ornamentation, and other qualities not found combined in other masonry materials."[2] These properties were superbly exploited by some of America's finest architects, including Louis Sullivan, Frank Furness, and Frank Lloyd Wright.

Polychrome glazed terra cotta was first introduced into American architecture in 1900 by McKim, Mead, and White in New York's famous Madison Square Presbyterian Church. Even with the enormous success of this outstanding example, strongly colored terra cotta remained an exception rather than the rule for the next two decades. Just prior to 1920, after a prolonged period of monochromatic terra cotta cladding, an upsurge of interest in color developed. This new attitude toward color — that it should stand out and attract the viewer's attention — became widespread. Polychrome terra cotta was introduced as an emphatic element in entryways, street level arcades, cornices, and lobbies. An enormous range of glazes was developed including fashionable "deco" shades such as lime-green, lavender, and ebony.

Although terra cotta appeared in a highly visible form in Art Deco architecture of the 1920s, during this same period another very different approach to the use of terra cotta was also widespread. Numerous architects, who continued to design in *traditional* historical styles, recognized the advantages of terra cotta and chose to incorporate it in their buildings. Besides being fireproof, lightweight, and economical, terra cotta was extremely popular because it could be made to mimic far more expensive building materials. Through the careful choice of textures and glazes, terra cotta could be disguised as granite, limestone, or marble, and only the most astute building professional could recognize what the material actually was. The manufacturers of terra cotta stressed the potential for varied surface finishes and introduced glazes like "Granitex" that recreated the color and texture of granite. Architects who chose to use terra cotta in this way — essentially as a *substitute* material — usually relied on Greek, Roman or Gothic styles of design.

Use of terra cotta for eclectic ornamental styles as well as for the streamlined look of Art Deco continued to be common throughout this period. The demands of deco for a new, flatter look led to the introduction of machine-extruded terra cotta units. These pieces, compared to the earlier more sculptural ones, required less hand labor and could be produced more economically. Not only was the terra cotta less expensive, but its quick installation reduced building costs even further. That versatility enabled it to become part of the growing era of skyscraper construction.

Until 1930, the 52-story terra cotta-clad Woolworth Building in New York was the world's tallest building. However, the rapidly increasing height of skyscrapers brought an end to the use of terra cotta as a cladding material for the structure's entire exterior surface. Instead, glazed terra cotta was used as a decorative element in entrances and on facades. Brick skyscrapers built in this period often used terra cotta in particularly innovative ways, combining it with glass, metal, mosaic tile, and even colored mirror. Because the earliest application of American terra cotta was in brick buildings, its return to them in the 1920s and 1930s is an interesting phenomenon. The material had gone full circle, although while terra cotta had been used in the 1880s to imitate stone or metal details in masonry buildings, terra cotta of the 1920s was intended to be eye-catching.

By 1886 the terra cotta industry had recognized the need to organize, and the Brown Association was formed in the New York area. It was followed by the Manhattan Materials Company in 1896 and the Terra Cotta Manufacturers Association in 1902. Finally, in 1911, the National Terra Cotta Society, which remained active until 1934, was created. A combination of factors accounts for the eventual decline of the National Terra Cotta Society as well as for the declining use of terra cotta in the 1930s. The president of Federal Seaboard Terra Cotta Company, E. V. Eskeson, wrote in the *Bulletin of the American Ceramic Society* in 1932, "The dream of the modern architect is to build houses entirely out of metal, glass, and cement. In this construction, brick, tile, or terra cotta has no place."[3] These new materials — reinforced concrete, steel and aluminum, glass in large panels — were truly mass-produced machine products. They were economical and available quickly in very large quantities. Terra cotta manufacture was too labor-intensive and consequently too costly to remain in widespread use. It required hand finishing, time for proper drying and firing, and care in shipping and installation. Ironically, in the 1880s, economy had been one of the selling points of terra cotta. At the time, it *was* labor-saving in comparison to the laboriously carved stone ornament which it was intended to replace.

One positive outcome of the Depression for the terra cotta industry was the widespread construction of public buildings through WPA programs. Artists, craftsmen, and designers joined forces in efforts to enrich the buildings of this period. Terra cotta was used for large-scale murals as well as for architectural ornament in numerous small public buildings. Large-scale terra cotta works included the sculp-

tures, fountains, and structures of the 1939 New York World's Fair. Post offices throughout the New York area as well as important buildings like the Municipal Building in Washington, D.C., used terra cotta for exterior ornament and murals.

World War II brought additional hardship to this already struggling industry. Peter Olsen, president of the Federal Seaboard Terra Cotta Company in 1944, wrote, "As to the factory, we are extremely limited in manpower and for that reason cannot work very efficiently. We have men who are one day working in the pressing shops, and the next day grinding and perhaps the day following are drawing kilns. This would all be overcome by having, say, twelve to fifteen of our old skilled men back."[4] Following the war, the terra cotta industry suffered yet another blow. With the passage of time, many early 20th-century terra cotta buildings had begun to show the serious problems that could result from improper installation and maintenance. All building materials serve best when used with adequate knowledge of their properties and possibilities. Satisfactory performance of masonry generally depends upon three factors (apart from the nature of the particular masonry material) — adequate support, proper anchoring or bonding, and protection from water infiltration. Although the durability of terra cotta had long been recognized, these three factors — particularly water seepage — caused a variety of material failures and its durability came under scrutiny. Where twenty-four companies had flourished in 1920, only seven remained in operation by 1947. These survivors tried to adapt terra cotta to the continuing changes in the building industry but most failed and went out of business.

Gladding, McBean & Company, however, continued to be active, surviving the 1950s and '60s by producing large quantities of sewer pipe along with occasional terra cotta projects. The outlook for Gladding, McBean & Company began to brighten in the late 1970s, and over the last ten years they have produced various types of architectural terra cotta to fill nearly 600 job orders. Not only has their factory been kept busy, but increasing demand for terra cotta has led to the recent formation of several new companies in various parts of the country. These include Boston Valley Terra Cotta in Hamburg, New York, MJM Studios in South Kearny, New Jersey, and Superior Clay Corporation in Pittsburgh, Pennsylvania. Ludowici-Celadon, Inc.

in New Lexington, Ohio, nationally recognized for its fine roof tile, has begun to produce architectural terra cotta as well.

This renewed interest can be attributed to several factors. One major development has been the recognition of our architectural heritage through the field of historic preservation. This has led to a great increase in carefully executed restoration and maintenance of older buildings. Intense interest in preservation has resulted in the founding of many local and nationwide preservation organizations, each with an arena of specific concerns. Friends of Terra Cotta, a national non-profit preservation organization, was formed in 1981. Its purpose has been to promote education and research in the history, preservation, and use of architectural terra cotta and related ceramic surfaces. Since terra cotta was such a popular building material, it is found on many older structures as cladding or in combination with brick. The vast majority of terra cotta presently manufactured is for replacement pieces used in the restoration of historic structures. Serious interest in historic preservation developed in America during the years following World War II, as the building boom began to actively threaten historic structures. In a 1941 study, 6,400 historic buildings were identified nationwide, but by 1963, only 3,840 of these remained. Continuing growth of the preservation movement on a city, state, and national level is encouraging, although at times it is difficult to reconcile the slowness of its growth with the rapid spread of massive new development projects across the country.

Another factor leading to terra cotta's growing resurgence is the reintroduction of color, surface pattern, and ornamentation into today's architecture. After many years of steel and glass structures, architects are now using a wider range of materials and have also begun to incorporate many rich and varied elements into their buildings. This has led to an exploration of the unique options that terra cotta offers. Robert Venturi, an architect who has incorporated terra cotta into some of his buildings, made the following observations about its use today: "Opportunities abound for using terra cotta for the sensual enrichment of architecture. It is a surface material for inside and out that promotes ornament — ornament involving color, pattern, and relief; ornament reinforcing structural or formal qualities; ornament as accent or delineation or as overall pattern.

Because of its easy repetitiveness and inherent refinement, terra cotta can be a means of creating small-scale articulation as a counterpoint to the big size of many of our buildings today: it is a way to bring back 'human scale' to our cities as well as color and ornament."[5]

Both the Friends of Terra Cotta and the National Building Museum in Washington, D.C. have offered artists and architects opportunities to investigate contemporary uses for architectural terra cotta. In 1985, the National Building Museum sponsored a "Terra Cotta Competition," which resulted in a traveling exhibition. In 1988, the Friends of Terra Cotta held an exhibition called "Firing the Imagination: Artists and Architects Use Clay," which included work from six collaborative teams of artists and architects. Experimentation with terra cotta will continue as clay artists become aware of the long-standing role that clay has traditionally played in architecture.

Terra cotta manufacturers welcome the opportunity to develop original designs, thereby reestablishing collaborative relationships among craftsmen, artists, and architects that have long existed in the industry. The complicated interactions among these professionals vividly comes to life in the remarkable letters and documents cited throughout Gary Kurutz' essay in *The Architectural Terra Cotta of Gladding, McBean.* This fascinating text is accompanied by a superb selection of visual images, including the powerful contemporary photographs of Mary Swisher and the fine archival drawings, photographs, and colored renderings which have been donated by Gladding, McBean & Company to the California State Library Special Collections at Sacramento. Through the accessibility of such architectural documents as these, we can look forward to an increasingly enlightened approach to the preservation of our extraordinary terra cotta heritage.

Susan Tunick 1989

[1] *Economist,* Volume XII, August, 1894, p.206.

[2] William Lockhardt, "Architectural Terra Cotta," *General Building Contractor,* January 1931, p.3.

[3] E. V. Eskesen, *Bulletin of the American Ceramic Society,* 1932.

[4] Letter from Peter Olsen, 1944.

[5] Robert Venturi, "Introduction," *Impressions of Imagination: Terra-Cotta Seattle,* 1986.

Montage of San Francisco Buildings Featuring Gladding, McBean Terra Cotta, by Gabriel Moulin, c.1930

Clay Pit, Lincoln

San Francisco Examiner columnist Ernest Hopkins wrote in July, 1928: "From a hole in the ground, here in the lower end of Placer County, the modern city of San Francisco has come."

Hopkins' striking words, in describing the influence of the terra cotta works of Gladding, McBean and Company, applied not only to San Francisco but also to every major city in the far West. Out of this rich deposit of clay in the foothills of the Sierra Nevada mountains came the terra cotta that clad and decorated thousands of buildings ranging from stately city halls to utilitarian warehouses.

From the 1880s to the 1930s, architectural styles ranging from Beaux Arts Classicism to Art Moderne used terra cotta as a principal medium for ornamentation and cladding because of its extraordinary plasticity, durability, variety of color, moderate price and its ability to complement marble, granite, and brick. During this era, terra cotta was featured in the most prominant buildings in San Francisco, Los Angeles, Sacramento, San Diego, Fresno, Portland and Seattle. The skylines of these young, growing urban centers were dotted with buildings sheathed in tan, gray and white "burnt earth."

Today many of these structures still survive as pleasant reminders of a time when architects and terra cotta companies collaborated to create imaginative buildings enlivened with lions, bears, eagles, gargoyles, and cherubs, and a seemingly endless variety of mythological figures and botanical specimens.

When architectural terra cotta enjoyed its heyday, the Placer County firm of Gladding, McBean and Company dominated the industry in California and the far West. The "pottery," as it was called, grew from a small concern specializing in sewer pipe to a far-flung building materials empire that survives today as the only remaining major producer of architectural terra cotta from that era. The story of its development, as documented through its pictorial archive and surviving records, portrays a company that literally shaped the urban landscape with ornamented buildings that still rank among the most admired in their respective cities.

The following narrates, in part, the history of this terra cotta works in Lincoln through several of its largest and most representative architectural projects in California, buildings that the company itself thought important as evidenced in its advertising and publications. Emphasis is given to San Francisco, Los Angeles, Sacramento, Oakland, and San Diego as these cities served as the sites for the vast majority of their architectural production. Excluded are Gladding, McBean projects in Seattle, Portland, Honolulu, Salt Lake City and Phoenix because these have, for the most part, been covered elsewhere. For the same reason, "in-depth" coverage is not given to the company's other products: roofing tile, sewer pipe, decorative tile, garden pottery and tableware. Further, this publication is not intended as a comprehensive company history chronicling corporate structure, profit and loss, and labor relations. Rather, the description of individual buildings and their terra cotta details will give the reader an insight into the inner workings of a major terra cotta works' architectural department: its relationship with architects, contractors and artists; techniques used in manufacturing; competition from other terra cotta companies, and the amazing variety of public and commercial buildings that challenged the ingenuity of the Lincoln artists and craftsmen.

Edward F. O'Day, editor of Gladding, McBean's house magazine *Shapes of Clay,* wrote a short history of the company for the April-May 1927 issue, narrating how this business "grew steadily and soundly" from modest beginnings in 1875 to become an international building empire. He boasted that the corporation's "products exhaust every conceivable 'shape of clay.' These are fired," he reported, "in 180 down-draught and four tunnel kilns. Its employees number more than two thousand. Its assets are over ten million dollars." Never one for understatement, O'Day went on to write, "The progress from sewer-pipe to terra cotta and numerous other lovely clay products has been an industrial march of beauty." He was not far off the mark. The business founded by three men from Chicago had expanded from its modest beginnings in Lincoln to a point where its manufacturing plants, sales rooms, sales yards, and clay pits held strategic positions from Vancouver, British Columbia, to Dallas, Texas. In the early 1920s the company absorbed Tropico Potteries of Los Angeles and greatly expanded its line of decorative tile for use in commercial projects and private residences.

While the use of Gladding, McBean's architectural products was concentrated in California, buildings incorporating its products rose throughout the Western United States and Canada. The pottery shipped terra cotta across the Sierras to the Nevada towns of Reno, Carson City, Elko and Las Vegas, and to Salt Lake City, Tucson, Phoenix, and Kansas City. Outside the continental United States and Canada, Lincoln terra cotta found its way to Honolulu, Tokyo and as far away as Sydney, Australia.

During the depression years of the 1930s, Gladding, McBean and Company suffered, but it survived because of its diversity of utilitarian clay products.

Gladding, McBean displayed amazing resilience in the 1930s as architectural styles evolved from the generously articulated historical themes to refined streamline facades and reliance on other materials such as stucco, cast stone and glass. The company answered this challenge by developing machine-made ceramic veneer and promoting its roofing tiles, face brick and Hermosa decorative tile. Projects funded by governmental agencies during this lean period kept the flagging architectural department alive. Versatile face brick provided a stable source of income, and Gladding, McBean roofing tiles, complementary to a number of architectural motifs, never waned in popularity.

Franciscan Ware became synonymous with the Gladding, McBean name during the 1930s. From Glendale in Southern California, the pottery began production of the famous tableware and art pottery in 1934. The first dinnerware consisted of plain shapes and bright colors recalling California's Hispanic past. Gradually other colors and shapes were added, and by the next decade, Franciscan Apple, Desert Rose, Ivy, Fruit and Poppy designs became commonplace in American households. In fact, Franciscan

John Breuner Company, Oakland

Ware gained such national prominence that the Metropolitan Museum of Art in New York invited the pottery to participate in its industrial exhibit. Additionally, Gladding, McBean factories mass produced art goods, kitchenware, flower pots and garden pottery. Thus, by the close of the decade, a typical California home could be protected by a Gladding, McBean tile roof, with walls composed of face brick, a kitchen and bathrooms surfaced in Hermosa tile, swimming pool lined with aquamarine tiles, a yard dotted with terra cotta flower pots and benches, and its occupants dining from Franciscan Ware.

Today the Lincoln architectural department is enjoying a renaissance. Because of its skill and experience, the company now receives orders to match terra cotta on buildings constructed over 50 years ago. Restorations of such famous edifices as the Wrigley Building in Chicago, Carnegie Hall in New York, and the Hotel Utah in Salt Lake City have enabled the Lincoln staff to revive techniques perfected in the early part of the century. As well, orders have been received to clothe buildings in terra cotta for high rises in San Francisco and Tulsa, Oklahoma, the prestigious Robert O. Anderson Building at the Los Angeles County Museum of Art, and for fashionable shops on Rodeo Drive in Beverly Hills.

Interest in the plant and its workings by preservation groups and architectural historians has led to a renewed appreciation for architectural terra cotta. Walking tours pointing out significant examples of architectural terra cotta in cities such as San Francisco, Sacramento, and Los Angeles have stirred a great deal of interest, and tour leaders speak with admiration of the artists and kiln masters of Lincoln. Plant tours, led by knowledgeable employees, leave visitors with a sense of awe, not only for the huge bee-hive kilns with their intense heat but also for the chance to walk through the long, dusty modeling and pressing rooms to see skilled workmen transforming Placer County clay into objects of great beauty. More than anything, however, looking upon the surviving molds, plaster casts and giant easels that were once used to produce the ornaments for some of California's finest buildings represents an unequalled architectural experience. To step into the office of Ernest Kadel, still as he left it in 1959, with its tables and walls still filled with old, curled photographs of past triumphs, evokes a feeling of reverence for the skill and pride of the Lincoln artists and artisans who beautified the streets and skylines of California and the West.

15

Easel with RCA Logo from Sherman-Clay Building in Los Angeles

16

Metropolitan Life Insurance Building, San Francisco

Sacramento Public Library   *Terra Cotta Details, Los Angeles*

17

Dome, Pantages Theater, Los Angeles

Today many of these structures still survive as pleasant reminders of a time when architects and terra cotta companies collaborated to create imaginative buildings enlivened with lions, bears, eagles, gargoyles, and cherubs, and a seemingly endless variety of mythological figures and botanical specimens.

Turn Verein Building, Sacramento

Pacific Gas & Electric Sub-station, San Francisco

Terra Cotta Detail, Sacramento Memorial Auditorium

19

Window Detail, Auditorium and Exhibit Hall, City of Pasadena, 1931

In the early 1920s the company absorbed Tropico Potteries of Los Angeles and greatly expanded its line of decorative tile for use in commercial projects and private residences.

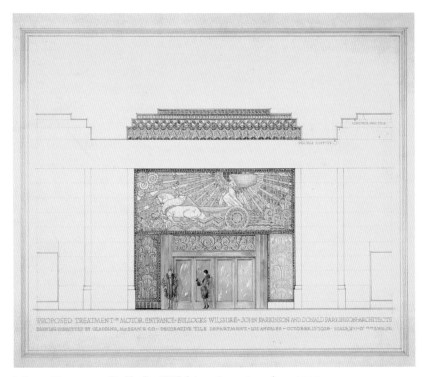

Motor Entrance, Bullocks Wilshire, Los Angeles, 1928

Mural Design for Chicago Yacht Club, 1930

Paramount Theater, Oakland

Proposed Decorative Panel and Seat, W. S. Fulton Museum, Dragoon, Arizona

Ernest Kadel's Office, Lincoln, 1988

Ernest Kadel's Office, Lincoln, 1911

Cupids on Turtles

Photo: Mary Swisher

Still Life with Ash Trays

Deer Head

Head of Athena and Shrinkage Rulers

Photo: Mary Swisher

Alter Cart, Glaze Room

Sonny in Beehive Kiln

Photo: Mary Swisher

29

Sunlight on Molds, Pressing Room

Plaster Mold on Cart

31

Della Robbia

Modeling Room, South Wall

33

Fireman's Fund Capital and Figures from the Los Angeles Athletic Club

Ruben Leon and Capital, Metropolitan Square Restoration, Washington, D.C.

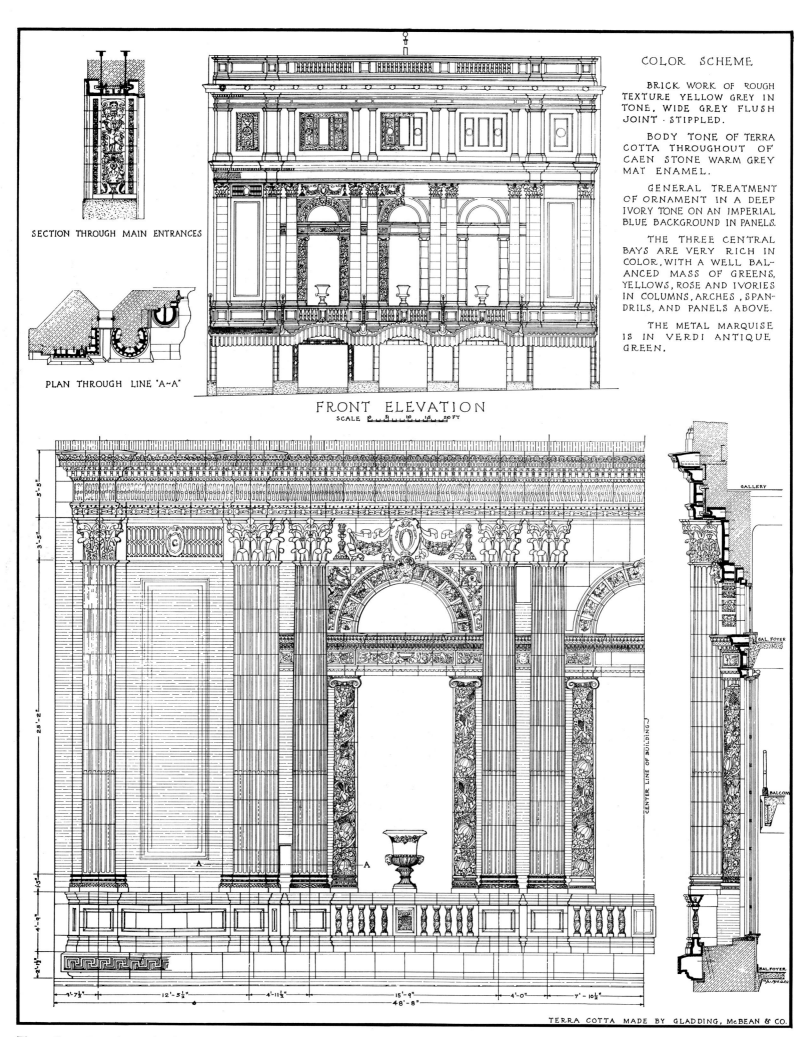

SECTION THROUGH MAIN ENTRANCES

PLAN THROUGH LINE "A-A"

FRONT ELEVATION
SCALE 0 5 10 15 20 FT

COLOR SCHEME

BRICK WORK OF ROUGH TEXTURE YELLOW GREY IN TONE, WIDE GREY FLUSH JOINT · STIPPLED.

BODY TONE OF TERRA COTTA THROUGHOUT OF CAEN STONE WARM GREY MAT ENAMEL.

GENERAL TREATMENT OF ORNAMENT IN A DEEP IVORY TONE ON AN IMPERIAL BLUE BACKGROUND IN PANELS.

THE THREE CENTRAL BAYS ARE VERY RICH IN COLOR, WITH A WELL BALANCED MASS OF GREENS, YELLOWS, ROSE AND IVORIES IN COLUMNS, ARCHES, SPANDRILS, AND PANELS ABOVE.

THE METAL MARQUISE IS IN VERDI ANTIQUE GREEN.

GALLERY

GAL. FOYER

BALCONY

BAL.FOYER

CENTER LINE OF BUILDING

TERRA COTTA MADE BY GLADDING, McBEAN & CO.

Terra Cotta Details, Columbia Theater, San Francisco, 1915

Drafting Room, Lincoln, 1921

Models for Panels, Hobart Building, San Francisco, 1914

38

Terra Cotta Being Installed on Upper Floors, Hobart Building, San Francisco, 1914

39

After the Fire, Gladding, McBean Plant, Lincoln, 1918

Terra Cotta Extruded Pipe, Lincoln, 1912

Lions for Metropolitan Life Insurance Annex, San Francisco, 1913

Removing a Clay Model from the Plaster Mold, Lincoln, c.1912

Orpheum Theater Detail, Los Angeles, 1911

Orpheum Theater Detail, Los Angeles, 1911

Stylized Stag Skull, Stability Building, Los Angeles, 1917

Base of Dome, Pantages Theater, Los Angeles, 1919

Entrance Arch, Hunter-Dulin Building, San Francisco, 1926

Work in Progress for Pantages Theater, Los Angeles, 1919

Detail for Pantages Theater, Los Angeles, 1919

First National Bank, Oxnard, 1917

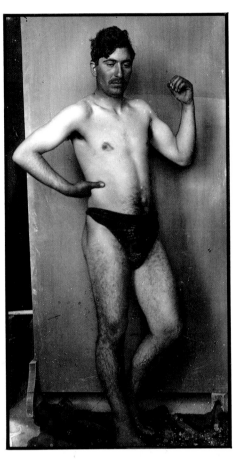

Plant Worker Used as Model, Lincoln, c.1915

Entrance Medallion, Turn Verein Building, Sacramento, 1925

Capital, Metropolitan Life Insurance Building, San Francisco, 1919

Eagle for First National Bank Building, Santa Rosa, 1920

Stock Column, Lincoln, c.1920

Capital, Fireman's Fund Building, San Francisco, 1914

Column Base, Fireman's Fund Building, San Francisco, 1914

Capital for Yolo County Courthouse, Woodland, 1916

Capital for Nippon Yusen Kaisha, Tokyo, 1921

Capital for Biltmore Hotel, Los Angeles, 1922

Capital for Japan Oil Company, Tokyo, 1920

Details for Jr. Orpheum Theater, San Francisco, 1920

Stock Columns, Lincoln, c.1920

Urn for Biltmore Hotel, Los Angeles, 1922

58

Urn for Nippon Yusen Kaisha Building, Tokyo, 1921

Sculpture by Carlos Tagliabue, 1926

Sculptor with Eagle, c.1915

Caryatids, c.1920

Loew's State Theater, San Francisco, 1920

Orpheum Theater, Kansas City, 1920

Store Front with Terra Cotta Details, Los Angeles, c.1912

Figures for Yolo County Courthouse, Viewed from Eye Level, Woodland, California, 1916

Figure for Hunter-Dulin Building, San Francisco, 1926

Hunter-Dulin Building, San Francisco, 1926

War Memorial Building, Chico, 1925

Biltmore Hotel, Los Angeles, 1922

68

Parker Lyon's Store, Los Angeles, 1922

Proposed Eagle for Pacific Telephone & Telegraph Building, San Francisco, 1924

Gargoyle for Knickerbocker Building, Los Angeles, 1913

Eagle for Pacific Telephone & Telegraph Building, San Francisco, 1924

Pacific Telephone & Telegraph Building, San Francisco, 1926

Cartouche for Ninth Floor, Matson Building, San Francisco, 1921

Matson Building, San Francisco, 1921

Rose Window, Sinai Temple, Los Angeles, by Tropico Plant; Norton & Wallis, architects; 1925–26

Terra Cotta Detail, Sacramento Memorial Auditorium   *Photo: Mary Swisher*

Sacramento Memorial Auditorium, 1927

79

Richfield Oil Building Under Construction, 1928

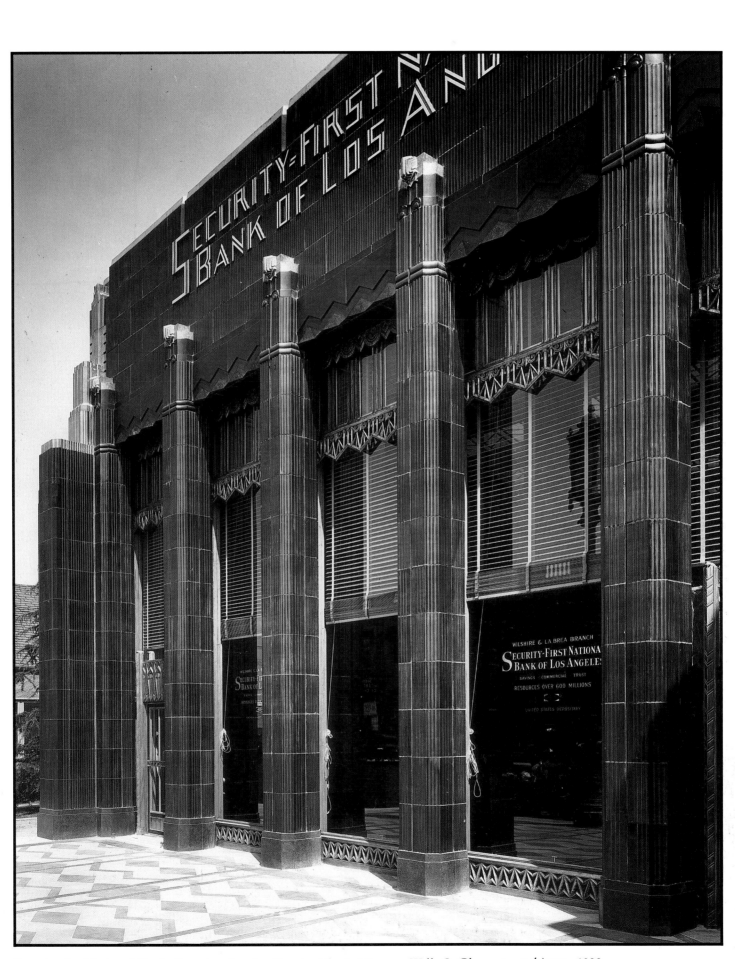

Security 1st National Bank, Los Angeles, by Tropico Plant; Morgan, Walls & Clements, architects, 1929

One-fourth Size Model for Los Angeles County Courthouse by Donal Hord, 1956

Full-size Detail of Bas-relief Panel

Terra Cotta Cladding on Los Angeles City Hall

Installation, Fort Moore Pioneer Memorial, Los Angeles, 1957

Ernest Kadel with Fort Moore Pioneer Memorial Clay Model, 1957

North Wall of Ernest Kadel's Office, 1981 Photo: Mary Swisher

SHAPES *of* CLAY

Gary F. Kurutz

Sometime in 1874 a Placer County road builder set out to straighten a country road between the Towle ranch and the town of Lincoln, about twenty-eight miles northeast of Sacramento. Cutting into a ridge, the builder accidentally discovered an unusually fine deposit of pure white kaolin clay. So important was this discovery and the earlier discovery of coal nearby that they made the newspapers of San Francisco. Charles Gladding, visiting from Chicago, read the San Francisco *Daily Alta California*'s notice of these discoveries and soon went up to Lincoln. There he obtained samples of the clay from the coal mine of Charles Lincoln Wilson, and tests proved that the substance was indeed of the finest quality. With the growth of West Coast cities and towns, Gladding anticipated a need for sewer and water pipe, chimney tops, brick, flower pots and other types of building products that could be created with the resources of the coal mine and clay pit. Apparently, at that point Gladding struck a deal with George Towle, owner of the clay pit, to test the feasibility of a clay products factory.

Enthusiastic over the test results, Gladding returned to Chicago and enlisted the help of Peter McGill McBean and George Chambers. Together, on May 1, 1875, they formed a partnership and called the new business Gladding, McBean and Company. The capital of the infant company was $12,000. All three men had been engaged in the building trades in the Chicago area and brought to the new company a wealth of experience. Gladding, a successful contractor, had established an extensive trade in the sale of sanitary ware and sewer pipe. McBean, prior to his arrival in California, worked as a building contractor in a family business and had also mastered the art of finance. The third partner, Chambers, was a highly respected engineer and contractor who had erected several of Chicago's early skyscrapers after the great 1871 fire.

Two weeks later, Gladding returned to California with his son Albert J. Gladding to begin the manufacture of vitrified sewer pipe. According to his son's recollections, an expert crew of workmen accompanied him to Lincoln, including Harry White, an experienced manufacturer of pipe. On May 12, the crew began the erection of a building and kiln and in June the necessary heavy machinery arrived. It consisted of a boiler, engine, pumps, steam press and roller crusher. Besides taking over one of the richest clay deposits in the world, the partners benefited by the location

of the little town of Lincoln. It was strategically located on the main line of the Oregon division of the Central Pacific Railroad. Thus, the task of shipping their products to the population centers did not pose a serious problem. Further, Lincoln was only a short journey from Sacramento and its river front embarcadero.

In the meantime, McBean moved to San Francisco and in August established a sales office and yard in the 1300 block of Market Street. The office gave prospective San Francisco customers an opportunity to view first hand the creations of the Lincoln plant. More adept at office details than Gladding, Peter McBean ran the business end of things, and San Francisco became the company's headquarters. The role of Chambers remains unclear as he apparently never moved to California. A man of considerable means, he lent his financial and engineering support from afar, and he remained a partner until his death in 1897.

Production of vitrified sewer pipe began in earnest, and by August 12, 1875, the Lincoln pottery sent its first carload down to McBean's San Francisco yard. On December 28, 1875, with bright prospects ahead, the partners entered into a ten-year lease with George Towle for the use of his clay pit. As compensation, Towle would get ten cents for every 2000 pounds of clay excavated.

Evidently, their vitrified pipe was well received, as they filled orders from such distant cities as Los Angeles, San Diego, Portland, Seattle, and Vancouver. As further evidence of prosperity, the company placed a full page advertisement in I. W. Taber's deluxe San Francisco business directory for 1880 and boasted that it had agents "at all points." According to the directory, Gladding, McBean and Company were manufacturers and dealers in "sewer pipe, chimney pipe, chimney tops, fire brick, fire tile, fire clay, terra cotta tile, fire clay, terra cotta garden vases, flower pots, chemical manufactures ware." The directory also included a photograph of their exhibit at the 1880 Mechanic's Fair that consisted of a forest of terra cotta and clay products.

To keep up with the sales force, the "manufactory" back in Lincoln expanded. Under Gladding's direction, the pottery works spread over two acres and included two huge buildings, five kilns and a sixty-horsepower stationary steam engine with two boilers. Workers in the clay pit nearby loaded the dry material into wagons drawn by mule-team to the Gladding, McBean plant. By 1883, seventy-five men and boys were employed in transforming the raw materials into high-demand building products. An article in the September 22, 1883, *Mining and Scientific Press* described the output of the factory as immense and its machinery as the best. An accompanying wood engraving depicted a bustling plant with smoke billowing from seven stacks, stockpiles of pipe and a Central Pacific train waiting alongside for the latest shipment. Stands of nearby "Digger Pine" provided hot-burning fuel necessary to heat the kilns to the required temperature. By 1888, the kilns consumed 10,000 cords of firewood annually.

In 1884, Gladding, McBean took a most significant step by further diversifying into manufacturing terra cotta for architectural ornamentation. Naturally, the first building to receive this treatment was their own. In June of that year, the firm erected a two-story building at 1358–1360 Market Street. Designed by architects Wright and Sanders and assisted by a draftsman experienced in terra cotta, the brick-faced structure was adorned with ornamental tiles, window sills, lintels, cornice and arches in light buff terra cotta, and even a terra cotta street and address panel, all manufactured in Lincoln. According to Charles Gladding's son Albert: "This was the first building erected on the Pacific Coast in which architectural terra cotta [was] used for trimmings, and it attracted much attention." An old photograph of the building shows that the firm shared space with a music company, Pilgrims Baptist Church, and the San Francisco Sewer Pipe Association.

The California Architect and Building News (November, 1884) contained a short article extolling the use of terra cotta and its superiority as a building material. "Architects and builders now realize that in terra cotta they have a material at once beautiful, imperishable, and far less costly than a poor quality of stone, when worked into architectural detail." The journalist went on to praise its versatility, ability to carry various tints and colors, compatibility with other materials and durability; he wrote that "any conceivable pattern can be made." It was no coincidence that the magazine referred its readers to Gladding, McBean & Company. The next two pages consisted of a company advertisement printed in clay colored ink showing off its architectural products including their own building as well as selected panels, friezes, tiles, and medallions.

Around this same time, the company began publishing its own advertising catalogs and, of course, devoted considerable space to "terra cotta in architecture." The writers articulated advantages of Gladding, McBean's products:

One of the most marked improvements connected with the building trade in this country during the past decade is the use of terra cotta for the purposes of architectural decoration. Ten years ago a majority of those engaged in the building trade did not know of its existence, so accustomed were they to simple brickwork, painted wood, or decoration in galvanized or cast iron.

Architects and builders now realize that in Terra Cotta they have a material at once beautiful, imperishable, and far less costly than a poor quality of stone, when worked into architectural detail. It is a material that will enable them to utilize and harmonize local materials.

We have spared neither time, money nor energy to enable us to offer the best quality of Terra Cotta that can be produced. The bodies of our wares are unexcelled for strength, beauty and durability.

Gladding, McBean had now successfully demonstrated the chief advantages of their product. Terra cotta, before being fired in a kiln, was soft and pliable and workmen could mold it into just about any shape. The architect could then inspect the full-size reproduction of the ornament while it was in this soft state and make any adjustments. As one company publicist said enthusiastically, terra cotta "is plastic in the hands of the architect." Further, once a mold was made, it could be used over and over. This feature represented a tempting alternative when compared to carving ornamentation in natural stone piece-by-piece or using pressed metal. Moreover, terra cotta ornamentation made of hollow blocks weighed considerably less than stone.

Pacific Coast architects, following eastern precedent, now demanded this versatile product, and Gladding, McBean was only too willing to meet the need. Acceptance of their Market Street building led to contracts for other buildings. That same year architects Wright and Sanders called upon them to manufacture terra cotta for the four-story Society of California Pioneers building in San Francisco. In mid-1885, the crew at Lincoln fabricated $4500 worth of clay ornamentation for the "Venetian-Gothic" style building. Pioneer Hall certainly represented their most artistic achievement and admirably demonstrated the plasticity of Lincoln clay. Highlights included busts of prominent pioneers and bas-relief panels depicting such historic scenes as the raising of the Bear Flag in Sonoma and pioneers crossing the plains. Noted New York sculptor F. Marion Wells produced the models and the molds for the project.

Buoyed by their success with Pioneer Hall and also with the Peter Donahue's Union Foundry Block, Gladding, McBean and Company incorporated on March 26, 1886. Charles Gladding served as president, George Chambers as vice-president, and Peter McBean as secretary and treasurer. After the death of his two associates in the 1890s, Peter became president. Interestingly, the sons of all three founders succeeded their fathers in the business. Peter's son Atholl later served as secretary and then as president during the golden age of terra cotta in the first part of the twentieth century. Albert Gladding eventually became first vice-president and managed the Lincoln plant; and Chambers' son George served as second vice-president.

While the company had attracted attention for its ornamental terra cotta, developments in architectural engineering swept them along into increasingly massive jobs. The advent of the skyscraper in Chicago and other eastern cities demonstrated that terra cotta represented a superior product not only for ornamentation but also for structural purposes. Tall buildings, made feasible by the elevator and steel frame construction, required a building material that was at once lightweight, fireproof, and malleable. San Francisco, then the commercial heart of the far West and surrounded by water on three sides, was a natural location for these Chicago style office towers and the products of the Lincoln kilns. Just as buildings began their skyward push, an individual of considerable importance joined the pottery in Lincoln.

Joseph Baldwin DeGolyer, a civil engineer with a specialty in chemistry, a son-in-law of Chambers, came to Lincoln in 1888 to assist the young corporation. Drawing on his own considerable talents, DeGolyer soon headed up the fledgling architectural department. At the time, this unit occupied 500 square feet and kept only one kiln busy. Under DeGolyer, the architectural operation expanded by the 1920s to 500,000 square feet, eighteen kilns and a work force of 300 men. Here the bespeckled DeGolyer directed everything from the drafting room to the modeling of clay to the packing of finished terra cotta in tule straw harvested

from the Sacramento delta. Making a careful study of the history and applications of terra cotta in the building trade, DeGolyer directed the creation of an extraordinarily diverse product line and such breakthrough developments as the development of polychrome finishes. During his tenure he oversaw the production of terra cotta for over 1800 buildings. A history of Placer County credited the chemist with transforming the pottery into one of the foremost producers of architectural terra cotta products in the country. The basis of the company's livelihood, however, remained the manufacture of sewer pipe and other more utilitarian materials.

The first important job that DeGolyer directed was M. H. DeYoung's ten-story Chronicle Building, San Francisco's first skyscraper and the first steel-frame building west of Chicago. It was designed by the Chicago firm of Daniel Burnham and John Root. The opportunity for a terra cotta works established by three Chicagoans to collaborate with such a prestigious architectural firm no doubt represented a tremendous boost in confidence. DeGolyer, after receiving the architects' drawings, then drafted the terra cotta decoration for the brick clad Romanesque-style Market Street building. According to the *California Architect and Building News,* Gladding, McBean produced $10,500 worth of ornamental terra cotta work and $36,000 worth of fire-proofing. For the latter, the pottery produced tons of hollow tile for use in partitions, floors, arches and as protection for steel and wooden columns. A *San Francisco Chronicle* reporter writing for the October 13, 1890 issue remarked how the lofty Chronicle building made San Franciscans shake their heads with wonder and doubt. Clearly Burnham and Root's Chicago School style had started a revolution in the West, and steel and burnt clay were their instruments.

In working on this building, DeGolyer established a pattern of work that governed the operation in Lincoln. Company correspondence indicated how important it was to meticulously follow the directions of the architect and to make every effort to please the client. Instructions generally came from the company's San Francisco office rather than directly from the architect. In Lincoln, DeGolyer and his colleagues kept careful records and recorded in leather bound volumes the details of the job. On the second floor of a sprawling building at the pottery, DeGolyer and his crew of draftsmen, sculptors and pressers put the architect's drawings into three-dimensional objects. The company magazine *Shapes of Clay* furnished an excellent description of the work performed on the Lincoln drafting room tables and in the modeling rooms:

When the architect's drawing reaches the drafting room at the factory, a key drawing is made which shows the location of the terra-cotta on the building. Thereupon, a scale outline, or shop drawing, is made, minutely following the architect's drawing. This shop drawing is submitted to the architect for his approval, and nothing further is done until that approval is forthcoming. The next step is to "put the work into the shop." Dimensions are checked both architecturally and structurally, and the setting number and the mold mark are given. Working drawings are then made in full size, with allowance for shrinkage, and after every piece has been carefully scheduled, the job is released from the drafting-room to the factory. In the plaster shop models and molds are produced from full-sized shrinkage details in conjunction with the working drawings. In the modeling-room artists of refined skill model the ornament. At every step of these processes the architect exercises the degree of control that seems necessary to him.

A great deal of original work is done in the modeling-room by sculptors on the staff of the Company. Their creative efforts are frequently called upon, and with very happy results. But here the architect's drawings pass through the same stages and are under his supervision exactly as in the drafting-room.

Burnham and Root followed up the success of the Chronicle Building with plans for another ten-story addition to the San Francisco skyline. Commissioned by the noted banker D. O. Mills, their design called for a steel-framed Romanesque tower with heavy use of terra cotta trim for the upper portions.

Once again, the architects contracted with Gladding, McBean. Located on Montgomery Street at Bush, the first two floors of the Mills Building were clad in Inyo marble and the remaining eight were clothed in Roman brick and gray-buff terra cotta. Strapped to the frame with iron were terra cotta medallions, rosettes, lion and griffin heads, belt courses in basket pattern, arabesques and heavily ornamented columns. Burnham and Root topped off the building with ornamented cornice and parapet pieces. Now ornamentation known only to the cathedrals and palaces of Europe was found on Pacific shores in the early 1890s.

Gladding, McBean and Company were proud not only

of their architectural ornamentation but also of their use of hollow tile for the floors, partitions, arches and columns. The pottery began manufacture of this innovative product in 1890. Certainly the weight of terra cotta when compared to stone offered a distinct advantage, but its manufacturers went to great lengths to tout the ability of hollow tile to withstand fire. Terra cotta hollow tile, stated its sales catalogs, offered absolute protection for wood, iron and steel columns. After all, materials fired in kilns had already been subjected to tremendous temperatures, much higher than any likely to be encountered in a building fire. Consequently, the pottery manufacturer and its architects claimed that buildings like the Mills and Chronicle were absolutely fire proof. The 1906 earthquake and fire would put terra cotta to its ultimate test.

Another product that served the company well was face brick. Many Romanesque revival buildings in the far West featured brick in tandem with terra cotta ornamentation. Lincoln manufactured face brick for the first time in 1891 for use on the Tacoma City Hall and also for the San Francisco homes of H. S. Crocker and William F. Herrin. In 1899, the pottery introduced an enameled brick for the rear walls of the Post Office and the court of the Flood Building. Face brick, because of its light colors, served to reflect light and brighten otherwise dull views. In the next century, when builders installed terra cotta as the primary clothing of the facade, face brick in matching colors was used for the rear and sides.

The Chronicle and Mills buildings represented proud accomplishments, but while these projects were underway, the terra cotta company's sales force continued to close deals across the Western landscape. As cities grew, so did Gladding, McBean's output of sewer pipe and water pipe, chimney caps, face brick, roof finials, stove linings, and garden pottery. Company products were being sold in every population center and its catalogs continued to list a growing number of buildings. Catalog Number 22, for example, supplied a list of eighty-two buildings found in twenty-nine cities. San Francisco dominated, but Los Angeles was the site for eight of their buildings. As a portent of the future, the Pacific Northwest proved receptive to the products of the Lincoln kilns. Fifteen structures graced Seattle and Tacoma and a half dozen rose above the streets of Portland. Typically, most architectural projects revolved around business blocks in downtown areas. The increased popularity of terra cotta, however, gained for the company contracts to furnish ornamentation for a variety of buildings including Southern Pacific Railroad depots, Masonic and Old Fellow halls, churches, schools, hotels, Wells, Fargo and Company buildings, court houses, post offices, theaters, homes for the well-to-do and buildings for St. Mary's College in Oakland, the University of California and Stanford University. The prosperity of the 1890s, based on such work orders, carried the company well into the next century.

Despite this growth, Gladding, McBean and Company found that it did not monopolize the terra cotta industry in California or the far West. By 1889, the Union Pressed Brick Company, with offices in San Francisco's Flood Building and its works in Vallejo, had already lured one important job away, the ten-story Crocker Building. Two other terra cotta works challenged the company's primacy in Northern California, Steiger Terra Cotta and Pottery Works and N. Clark and Sons. All won contracts for prestigious jobs and for many years competed vigorously for the favor of the architectural community and their patrons. Steiger, for example, produced the architectural terra cotta for the Grant, Monadnock and Rialto Buildings and the domed Humboldt Savings Bank in San Francisco. A cataclysmic fire on March 8, 1917, destroyed their South San Francisco plant and drove them out of business. Nathaniel Clark, with valuable clay deposits near Carbondale in Amador County and a large plant at West Alameda, produced ornamentation for the Union Depot, Clift Hotel, Foxcroft Building and St. Ignatius Church in San Francisco, Federal Realty Building in Oakland, and County Court House in Sacramento. N. Clark & Sons remained the Lincoln company's chief competitor in Northern California until it closed its doors in 1952. In the Pacific Northwest, three Washington companies, the Denny-Renton Clay and Coal Company of Seattle, Northern Clay Company of Auburn and Washington Brick, Lime and Sewer Pipe Company of Spokane did the lion's share of business.

To keep their products before the public eye, Gladding, McBean continually advertised in local media. Western newspapers, business directories, and architectural periodicals like *The California Architect and Building News* and *The Architect and Engineer of California* constantly carried their advertisements, and a regular succession of artfully designed catalogs reminded architects and contractors of their skill, diversity, and ability to meet any requirement. One of the most prestigious ways to curry favor in the trade was through the annual Industrial Exposition of the Mechanics' Institute in San Francisco. For many years the pottery entered an exhibit and in 1890 earned the coveted Grand Silver Medal for the best exhibit of architectural terra cotta. The awards committee which included two architects commended the company by writing:

We have much pleasure in drawing special attention to the excellent exhibit of Gladding, McBean & Co., showing as it does, marked enterprise as well as laudable and successful effort to establish in California a very notable industry, and displaying considerable perfection, both in technical and artistic qualities of the work produced, which in our opinion ranks with much of the best work produced in the Eastern United States and Europe.

As was often the case, Gladding, McBean and its western competitors looked to the East for inspiration and as a standard. Over the years modelers, chemists, and management staff employed by the company had often worked at one of the large terra cotta works in the Chicago or New York area before coming west. The Atlantic Terra Cotta Company in New York City, Northwestern Terra Cotta Company in Chicago, St. Louis Terra Cotta Company, Western Terra Cotta Company in Kansas City and Denver Terra Cotta Company, among others, dominated the trade in their respective regions. Occasionally, some won contracts for buildings as far away as British Columbia, Utah, and Texas. Logistical difficulties of time, distance, and control, however, generally prevented more established eastern firms from competing for jobs along the Pacific Coast.

Even with keen local competition, the San Francisco office continued to win substantial jobs, and the kilns in Lincoln continued to churn out quantities of terra cotta. Catalog Number 30 (circa 1900) listed 108 buildings, with nearly half in San Francisco. To give prospective clients a taste of their capabilities, Gladding, McBean embellished its catalog pages with photographs of various ornaments and an assortment of completed buildings including the U.S. Post Office and Court House and the Mills Building.

Terra cotta sustained its popularity because of the support of the architectural establishment and the patronage of

moguls who could afford to finance monumental buildings festooned with terra cotta ornamentation. According to Gary Knecht in his unpublished essay "Early Use of Architectural Terra Cotta in the San Francisco Bay Area," the architectural firm of the Reid Brothers and the wealthy Spreckels family ranked among the most enthusiastic proponents of terra cotta. Prior to the 1906 cataclysm, the Reids designed several important buildings for the Spreckels, and Gladding, McBean supplied the terra cotta.

Rising eighteen stories above San Francisco was the Claus Spreckels Building, at the corner of Third and Market. It housed the offices of the *San Francisco Call,* one of the city's leading newspapers. When it was completed in 1898, architectural critic B. J. S. Cahill lauded the steel framed skyscraper as the "handsomest tall office building in the world." The Reid Brothers clad the first 16 stories with sandstone but crowned the building with a magnificent Baroque style terra cotta dome. For many years this grand terra cotta dome stood out as the city's dominant architectural feature and was imitated widely. An article in the December 19, 1897, *Call* featured their new building and had this to say about the contribution of Gladding, McBean, and the use of terra cotta:

To the pedestrian on Market Street walking in the direction of the Spreckels Building and whose eyes rest lingeringly upon the beautiful dome which crowns the stately structure, the impression is conveyed that it is constructed of solid stone. This, however, is an error, for it is terra cotta, a material the use of which for practical purposes has become general among those who have to do with the construction of large buildings. The extensive use of terra cotta for architectural decoration has been very marked during the past few years and it is now recognized as a fire proof material of beauty, strength and durability.

The terra cotta work on the dome was performed by Messrs. Gladding, McBean & Co., . . . The material produced here [in Lincoln] is of the best and its works are extensive.

The steel work on the dome was carefully filled in with a covering of porous terra cotta, known as "fire proofing." Over this was laid the smooth finished terra cotta in small blocks accurately joined, so as to give the impression of being a continuous piece traversing the lines of the dome. The beauty of the work as well as its serviceability can be seen at a glance, and it reflects credit upon the contractors.

While the Reid Brothers gained recognition for adorning the streets of San Francisco's business district with monumental buildings, they also created mansions befitting the stature of the Spreckels family. Their most visible achievement was the home of John D. Spreckels at Pacific and Laguna Streets constructed in 1898 and 1899. Situated on the crest of a hill with a choice view of San Francisco Bay and Marin County, the home was designed in the grandiose manner of a French palace. At first glance, the three-story flat-roofed structure appeared to be made entirely of white marble. But for this commission, the architects asked Gladding, McBean to produce cream white terra cotta (Shade No. 205) for the entire facade from the foundation to the top of its "noble balustrade." The Spreckels mansion stood out as convincing testimony that DeGolyer and his staff could shape Lincoln clay into any desired form. They had created a facade that appeared as though quarried in Italy. Surprisingly, the Spreckels mansion was one of the few residences in San Francisco to make such liberal use of terra cotta. In the future, architects used fired clay sparingly for residential cornices, balustrades and window decoration and not as the principal clothing.

The use of $54,000 worth of cream white terra cotta for this ostentatious building highlighted an important trend for the pottery. In its earliest days in this country, terra cotta ornamentation mostly carried natural unglazed colors of red or salmon and blended well with the brownstone and brick of the Romanesque era. If a client wanted color, workers simply painted it on. With the 1893 Chicago Exposition and its celebrated "White City," architects ushered in a new generation of classical buildings clad in brilliant white glazed terra cotta. This development caught on in San Francisco and by the late 1890s relatively drab earthtones gave way to light colors; and, in subsequent decades, terra cotta chemists developed a variety of colors and glazed surfaces.

In April 1906, when San Francisco was rocked by an earthquake and decimated by fire, the entire building community was forced to reevaluate its design concepts and materials use. Terra cotta, long touted as "absolutely fireproof" by Gladding, McBean and its competitors, did not meet the test.

Although the terra cotta did not actually burn, the intense heat generated by the burning buildings caused hollow floor tiles to collapse. In several instances, terra cotta column covers cracked and consequently failed to

protect vulnerable steel and iron support columns from buckling. Ironically, Gladding, McBean's corporate headquarters on Market Street was lost during the conflagration, along with dozens of their other jobs.

Nonetheless, this disaster proved to be a boon for the building industry as San Francisco emerged from the rubble. Gladding, McBean and scores of others willingly stepped forward to help the city rebuild. By this time, terra cotta had become widely accepted by architects as an alternative to wood and stone, and the public apparently loved its versatile visual effects. Just as Chicago rose from the ashes by building skyscrapers clad in terra cotta in the 1870s, San Francisco responded in a similar manner after 1906. Moreover, city officials took corrective action with the building code to make sure terra cotta lived up to its fire proof claims. The new code required terra cotta column covers to be 4 inches thick rather than the pre-1906 thickness of only 1.5 inches.

The destructive forces of the fire and its aftermath also gave impetus to a heavier reliance on reinforced concrete. A building with reinforced concrete floors and concrete column protection, when combined with terra cotta, offered maximum fire protection.

Despite the incursion of poured concrete as a popular building material, architects relied on architectural terra cotta more than ever by using it as a veneer to relieve an otherwise dull facade. Previously, terra cotta was made primarily for ornamentation or trim. Now architects demanded a light-weight, fire resistant, weather-proof, easy to clean sheathing. Weighing considerably less than stone, terra cotta saved money on large buildings because it required less structural steel. It saved time, too, because masons could quickly attach it to the frame. When glazed, terra cotta remained relatively impervious to dust and pollutants, and with a good rain its surface again sparkled. Terra cotta works like Gladding, McBean responded to this new demand by manufacturing terra cotta in large flat blocks known to the trade as ashlar. Produced by the ton with the use of standard molds, terra cotta ashlar could be made to resemble just about any common building stone. For the next three decades, architects usually specified a base of granite, marble or limestone and finished the remaining stories with less expensive terra cotta ashlar made to match. As the company put it, "we saw an opportunity to outstone stone."

An important example of post 1906 construction was the Hearst Building at the once famous "Newspaper Angle" on Market and Third Streets. Designed by the New York firm of Kirby, Petit, and Green and constructed in 1909, this new facility for the *San Francisco Examiner* incorporated several features based on knowledge gained in the earthquake and fire. In considering outside walls, the architects selected materials known for their fire-resisting qualities, color, durability, availability and ease of being secured to the superstructure. Gladding, McBean's glazed terra cotta met all these criteria, and the company received the contract for much of the exterior treatment. An article in *The American Architect* (January 1908) by the architects' engineer, Charles Nichols, reflected this new found sensitivity to seismic concerns and the need to still present a pleasing facade:

The first and second stories will be faced with pink Tennessee marble, thoroughly anchored to the reinforced concrete backing. The facing from this point to the sixteenth floor will be white glazed terra-cotta. Above this floor the terra-cotta facing will be polychromatic. Each individual piece of terra-cotta is thoroughly anchored to the reinforcement and backed with concrete, making it impossible to dislodge. The loggia extending through the seventeenth and eighteenth floors will give varying deep shadows from the wide overhanging copper cornice, and together with the varicolored terra-cotta introduced at this point, produced an effect artistic in its result and differing from the monotonous facade of the usual commercial building.

While terra cotta did have its advantages, the Hearst Building demonstrably reflected a lack of confidence in hollow tile for floors, wall partitions and column protection. Concrete, plaster and wire mesh were selected instead. "It will be noted," wrote Nichols, "that brick work and terra cotta fireproofing have been entirely eliminated."

At the same time another development occurred that Gladding, McBean quickly rushed to capitalize on — the advent of polychrome or varicolored finishes. In this area DeGolyer led the way. An expert chemist, he introduced dozens of color variations into the company's palette. The company soon offered a wide selection of full and matte glazed terra cotta. Architects favored the matte glazed surface which was similar in texture to smooth but unpolished marble. Some criticized the shiny, polished full glaze as

being too bright for large buildings. Thus the company and the entire terra cotta industry, as mentioned earlier, began to offer clients more than traditional earthtones, and soon the skylines of the western urban centers were dotted with white and gray terra cotta facades and adorned with glazed ornaments in greens, reds, blues, whites, yellows, and golds. The stately Hearst Building served as a highly visible advertisement for this new product.

Following the loss of its Market Street building in the 1906 fire, Gladding, McBean and Company located its headquarters on the southwest corner of Eddy and Hyde Streets. After the city was rebuilt, the company moved into the Crocker Building where it remained during the bustling decades of the 1910s and 1920s. Warehouse facilities were maintained at Minna and Natoma before and after 1906.

Post-1906 San Francisco began the golden age of terra cotta on the Pacific Coast. Heavily influenced by the Beaux Arts school which emphasized historical or classical motifs, local architects designed a new series of office towers that took full advantage of the remarkable plasticity and color tones of terra cotta. As mentioned above, the Hearst Building gave the company an excellent opportunity to rebound with one of the city's most imposing new structures. Agents for Gladding, McBean also secured contracts for dozens of projects including such prominent buildings as the Balboa Building on Market Street, University Club on Nob Hill, Newhall Building on the corner of California and Battery Streets, the Renaissance/Baroque Southern Pacific Building at 1 Market Street, the delightfully narrow Heineman Building on Bush Street, and the music stand in Golden Gate Park. Under the strong leadership of Peter McBean and his son Atholl, the company worked with the principal architects of the day including Bliss and Faville, Lewis P. Hobart, A. Page Brown, James C. Green and Willis Polk.

At about this same time, Peter McBean added to his staff a head modeler of considerable talent, Pio Oscar Tognelli. Born in Italy in 1880 and trained at the Academia delle Bellearti in Florence, Tognelli was instrumental in executing quality models for sophisticated Beaux Arts style capitals, pilasters, panels, friezes, cartouches, gargoyles and other ornaments that decorated scores of buildings not only in San Francisco but also the entire length of the West Coast. Because of his considerable talents and responsibilities, he

was in frequent contact with the front office and eventually, in the 1920s, moved to San Francisco as head of the company's art department. It proved vital to have a man of Tognelli's skill and versatility because architects on occasion gave the factory only a general idea of what they wanted or simply referred them to a book on Italian architecture. Tognelli, in turn, received support in Lincoln from a staff of artists who carried out the more routine aspects of modeling.

To assist the architects in their work, the modeling department introduced photography into their operating procedure. Once the sculptors completed a model, staff placed the clay object on a massive easel and photographed it with a dry plate camera. Contact prints were made in a tiny darkroom, then sent to the architect for his approval or suggested modifications. This innovation frequently saved the architect the inconvenience of having to make a trip to distant Lincoln.

Workers employed at Lincoln found that many other aspects of the work had changed since the pioneer era. In place of reliance on human sweat and mule power, monstrous steam shovels mined the clay in step-like benches and, beginning in 1908, a narrow-gauge railroad with a locomotive pulling five-ton dump cars delivered the terra cotta clay to a covered shed at the plant. There a four-ton travelling crane lifted the material to appropriate bins and mechanical "pugging" machines. Another locomotive took waste terra cotta off to a dump for recycling as grog. Further, wood no longer fired the down-draft kilns used for terra cotta as the plant switched to crude oil. The once extensive stands of pine around Lincoln had disappeared into Gladding, McBean's kilns.

While the pottery employed its own sculptors for modeling ornamental works, the architect or his client periodically commissioned an independent artist. Such was the case with the Native Sons of the Golden West building on Mason Street, constructed in 1911. Following an Italian Renaissance motif, architects Righetti and Headman made liberal use of terra cotta. The Native Sons, however, wanted a more local flavor incorporated into the building so they hired the noted California sculptor and illustrator Jo Mora to create a series of bas-reliefs depicting scenes important in California history. In a case like this, the pottery's own modelers assisted by instructing Mora in the properties and limitations of terra cotta and producing full-size molds from his models.

Late in 1913, President McBean secured a contract to supply the terra cotta for the Hobart Building on Market Street near Montgomery. Commissioned by the Hobart Estate Company and designed by Willis Polk, its plan called for twenty stories and a penthouse. Earlier that year Polk had contracted with Gladding, McBean to produce the terra cotta for his Insurance Exchange Building on California Street. Copies of correspondence from Secretary Atholl up to Lincoln demonstrate his sales ability as well as the inner workings of the pottery. In January, Atholl convinced Polk's company to clad the entire facade of the Hobart Building in terra cotta. This required the hiring of two additional draftsmen. In a letter dated January 7, 1914, the company's president revealed, "We have had to take this contract at practically no profit. We took it simply to help us keep going until new business develops."

Under Polk's generalship, the Hobart Building rose at a record pace and under budget. On May 1, 1914, the Lincoln works sent its first carload of terra cotta to San Francisco and during that month sent a carload every day. No doubt the draftsmen, modelers, pressers, kilnsmen, and packers worked at a feverish pace in Lincoln. Every effort was made to please Mr. Polk, but occasionally Atholl admitted that the cost-conscious architect forced them to the limit. "We are going to put this job through the shop," wrote Atholl to DeGolyer, "on the very cheapest basis possible. We will only make replacements for such pieces that are badly chipped or broken; everything else will have to go. Mr. Polk has forced us to the last dollar; now we will have to force the job to make a profit out of our cost."

McBean also tried to persuade Polk to visit Lincoln to inspect the work of his modelers as they churned out the heavy and elaborate ornamentation that crowned his oval-shaped tower. However there is no record that Polk made the journey. For the finishing touch, the pottery supplied 2000 green glazed tiles for the penthouse. The work of DeGolyer's men occasionally elicited humorous candor from Atholl McBean. He chided his department head with the following memo: "You made a fatal mistake in applying the gold on two places. Mr. Polk is so pleased with it that he insists that we gild the top rib, also the edges of the flat ornament — suppose we will have to stand for it — so get this work under way at once."

Meeting the breakneck pace set by Polk, the Lincoln works set off its last shipment on July 1, 1914. Six hundred and fifty tons of matt enamel terra cotta stretching from the tip of the second story lintels to the chimney coping graced the handsome tower. The end result was, according to architectural historian Michael R. Corbett, one of the most unique skyscrapers in the country and one of Polk's favorite buildings.

Pleased with this striking addition to the skyline, Polk contributed an article to *The Pacific Coast Architect* (November, 1914) chronicling and explaining how such a massive building rose so quickly. Curiously, the architect made only one reference to terra cotta and did not mention Gladding, McBean once. This lack of recognition, however, was indicative of the relationship between designer and contractor. Only through a company advertisement in the same issue of the magazine did the reader have any idea of the collaborative effort.

Willis Polk inspired Cordova roofing tile, one of the pottery's most lucrative products. Since 1893, Gladding, McBean had manufactured roofing tile for scores of buildings including the original quadrangle at Stanford University. This early tile was characterized by its uniformity of color and gave buildings the appearance of having a painted roof. In 1913, Polk returned from Spain and other Mediterranean countries filled with enthusiasm for their picturesque and colorful tile roofs. He approached Peter McBean and asked the company to replicate these "Latin tiles" in a modern medium. Through extensive experimentation in the chemistry laboratories and kilns of Lincoln, the staff created a tile which they dubbed "Cordova." Cordova tiles were made in a wide range of colors including russett-browns, tans, purples and rose shades. By skillful installation, this variegated tile took on the appearance of an irregular ruglike texture that contemporary architects admired and soon demanded. Cordova and the related Mission, Escalona and Italian Pan styles were ready made for a region enthralled by Mission Revival and Renaissance architecture. Embraced by the building trade, Gladding, McBean roofing tile revolutionized the industry and catapulted the company into new markets not only in the West but also in the eastern United States and as far away as New Zealand.

Throughout the remainder of the decade, McBean's Lincoln works produced tons of terra cotta brick, ashlar and ornamentation for San Francisco. Other noteworthy buildings number the San Francisco City Hall, Fireman's Fund Insurance Building, Cowell Building, Bullock and Jones, and Masonic Temple. For the Public Library building in the civic center, DeGolyer and staff developed a coated brick appropriately named "Library Gray."

From his busy San Francisco office, Secretary Atholl McBean ran the production end of the company with an iron hand. His constant stream of memos and directives from the Crocker Building to Lincoln demonstrate his attention to detail and ability to motivate his far-flung staff. For example, during the construction of the Fireman's Fund Building, he excoriated Lincoln for improperly packing the pilasters on the railroad cars, as some arrived chipped. On the other hand, he praised them for producing some of the most beautiful terra cotta ever made.

Working directly with the architect provided Atholl McBean with a constant trial. Frequently architects complained that shipments had chipped or damaged pieces or that the color of the finished product did not match the original selection. McBean constantly advised his staff to follow the architect's instructions but also realized that their demands cost the company money. McBean cautioned Lincoln as the negotiations for the Fireman's Fund Building progressed: "We will not put any work in the shop until we have formal approval from the architect in writing. We cannot afford to have a row with the architect as we always pay the bill."

Occasionally, buildings required remodeling or expansion. The Metropolitan Life Insurance Company building near the summit of Nob Hill ranks as one of the most compelling examples. Originally built in 1909 and clad in rich matte-glazed white terra cotta, the spectacular neo-Classical structure was scheduled for an expansion program beginning in 1919. Gladding, McBean received a contract to supply the terra cotta. The pottery had already been involved in one such project in 1913. For this new addition, the huge insurance company hired J. R. Miller as the architect and James Furlong as the general contractor.

While the Lincoln staff had been called upon to execute such complicated tasks as replicating the polychrome frieze, the majestic pediment over the door was a special challenge. As with the Native Sons building, the client commissioned an independent sculptor, and the relationship between the artist and pottery provided a fascinating insight into the real life trials of the terra cotta business.

On May 22, 1919, Atholl McBean wrote DeGolyer in Lincoln that noted San Francisco sculptor Haig Patigian had been hired to do the pediment sculpture. McBean further explained that Patigian preferred to make quarter sized models to shrinkage scale and wanted the Lincoln staff to point it up rather than to make a full sized model. To assist with the process, Atholl suggested that the company's chief modeler Pio Tognelli meet with the sculptor and explain the limitations of terra cotta. At this point, the pediment work seemed to be progressing well.

A memo dated January 16, 1920, indicated, however, that the front office in San Francisco was growing impatient with the artist. "I took up with Mr. Patigian yesterday regarding the scale model of the pediment," wrote Atholl, "and he is a pretty impossible person to get anything definite from." In the meantime, the Lincoln staff suggested that Patigian visit the pottery but this, too, caused frustrations. Another lengthy memo stated: "Mr. Patigian informed Mr. Miller [the architect] this morning that he 'might possibly be able to appear in Lincoln Thursday morning to inspect the central feature of the pediment group.' Mr. Miller has made the statement that if Mr. Patigian did not materialize on that date, we would manage without him."

Correspondence in the company's files on this project show that the pottery failed to please Patigian. A letter from the sculptor dated May 17, 1920, roundly criticized Lincoln and defended his own performance. This letter superbly articulates the modeling process and what could go wrong. Patigian, his pen filled with vitriol, wrote to Miller:

Referring to photo of the second enlarged section of the Metropolitan Life Insurance Company's pediment sculpture, I find that the work done so far is sorely disappointing. The section in question is the one which shows a woman with two children and dog. The anatomical drawings are badly reproduced and the hand, wrist and foot of the woman, as well as the head and other details of the piece are sadly unlike the original.

Secondly, when Mr. Robert Payne was engaged to do the enlarging, I was very much pleased, seeing that Mr. Payne had vast experience in this work as he enlarged numerous pieces of the Panama-Pacific International Exposition statuary with the aid of an enlarging machine of his own invention . . . but he had been handicapped by different situations. First, I was given to understand that the model would be enlarged in modeling clay which would be cast in sections and the terra cotta clay was to have been pressed into the mould. This process was changed by the Gladding, McBean Company, obviously, to save time and money, and Mr. Payne was induced to do his work directly in terra cotta clay . . . thick and impossible material.

After the work was begun, an ornamental modeler employed at the Gladding, McBean factory was ordered to assist Mr. Payne in the work of enlarging. This person, I found out later, took liberties with the original design, criticizing the size or proportions here and there — suiting himself and distorting the work.

Summing up the situation, I can't help put the blame on the Gladding, McBean Company . . . and I am sorry to say that I have noticed a lack of respect on their part for an original work.

Despite all this complaining, contractor and artist managed to cooperate well enough to finish the job. In fact, Harry Noyes Pratt in the *Overland Monthly* called the pediment, with its heroic figures symbolic of the insurance industry, Patigian's most important work. The pottery staff preserved the artist's models for display in the rooms of the San Francisco Architectural Club and pointed with pride to their work on the tympanum group.

In July 1918 the company was dealt a severe blow when fire ravaged the Lincoln plant. And since Gladding, McBean employed over 600 men, the fire staggered the entire town. The fire swept through the main factory buildings consuming the brick, tile and sewer pipe operations, company offices, and nearly all the heavy machinery. Fortunately, the heroic volunteer fire fighters of Lincoln managed to save the architectural terra cotta department, kilns and towering smokestacks.

Despite this blow and a general production slow down caused by World War I, the pottery and its town rebounded. The economic significance of the terra cotta works was not lost on the community. In an article that appeared in the May 8, 1919, Lincoln *News Messenger,* the reporter recognized the company's contribution to the town:

It is the great clay producing factory of Gladding, McBean & Co. that has made Lincoln the biggest and best little city beautiful in California and the people in general here . . . will hail with joy the increasing activity at the big plant.

In fact, all that makes Lincoln one of the busiest little cities and one of the best places to live in all California, may be attributed very largely to Gladding, McBean & Co. And we didn't mention the magnificent water system . . . and the splendid sewer system which has made Lincoln one of the most healthful places in all California. Hats off to Gladding, McBean.

With the plant rebuilding and the restart of construction projects delayed by the war, the pottery embarked upon a new era of growth which, of course, meant prosperity for the company town of Lincoln. As another article in the local newspaper put it: "When the pottery is busy Lincoln is lively, and most of the pretty homes have been built directly through the monthly payroll of Gladding, McBean & Co." The newspaper happily announced J. B. DeGolyer's call for pressers, mold makers, kiln setters and general helpers to respond to the crush of jobs sent up from the San Francisco offices.

Back in San Francisco, the architectural community began drawing up plans for a new generation of high rise office buildings. Gladding, McBean & Co., N. Clark and Sons, and dozens of other manufacturers of building materials competed for these jobs. The Lincoln works, during the 1920s, landed several of the most massive and challenging of these projects. The Gothic style Robert Dollar Building, designed by Charles McCall, represented the first of these skyscraper projects for the pottery and set the pace of the next decade. It was a time of feverish activity as the company worked on several huge jobs simultaneously not only in San Francisco but also up and down the Pacific Coast.

During the boom decade of the 1920s, the pottery became more public-relations conscious and opened elegantly appointed show rooms in San Francisco and the leading cities of its far-flung territory. Company executives also placed full-page advertisements in the principal architectural magazines reminding architects of what their Lincoln kilns produced. As an additional communications device, Gladding, McBean began the publication of a magazine devoted to terra cotta bearing the picturesque name of *Shapes of Clay.* First issued in April, 1925, and edited by journalist Edward F. O'Day, the glossy magazine primarily featured company products and their noteworthy buildings and was distributed to architects, contractors and those interested in the building trade. Filled with the hyperbolic language of the day, it was published monthly and then quarterly until the 1930s. Despite its florid prose, *Shapes of Clay* served admirably to tell the story of terra cotta in California and provided superb documentation on the pottery's most important architectural projects. For example, a caption for a double-page photograph of the San Francisco skyline by Gabriel Moulin in 1927 glowingly summarized the extraordinary effect of the company and its product:

San Francisco, the Sky-Scraper Community of the West, Challenges the Beauty of the Sky with the Colorful Loveliness of Terra-Cotta. Gladding, McBean & Co., has fabricated the terra-cotta, to say nothing of roof tile and other clay products, for the outstanding structures of this noble sky-line. Among these are the Russ, Hunter-Dulin, Telephone, Standard Oil, P.G. & E., and Matson buildings.

San Francisco's skyline did indeed confirm O'Day's exuberant words, and all of the above mentioned buildings still grace the financial district. The first major Gladding, McBean terra cotta skyscraper of the 1920s was the fifteen story Matson Building at the southwest corner of Main and Market streets. Designed by the noted firm of Bliss and Faville, the Italian Renaissance structure followed a plan common to buildings of that era: base, shaft and top.

From the outset, the architects incorporated into the design symbols that reflected the interests of this important maritime concern. According to *Shapes of Clay,* this skyscraper "was designed in and for terra-cotta, the architects regarding that plastic material as most suitable to their interpretation of a business linked to ocean romance." The entire facing consisted of enameled gray-toned ashlar and column, while the piers and ornaments were made of polychrome and the background in "seagreen" terra cotta. Even the roof tile was made with a seagreen glaze.

Gladding, McBean actually began working on the building sometime in November 1921. Atholl McBean sent off a memo to Lincoln informing the staff that the contract had been awarded. Very pleased, McBean wrote: "It will all be terra cotta, according to the plans which you have, in color #10707. Polychrome colors to be decided by Mr. Bliss after he looks over the samples."

The instructions of Atholl to Lincoln concerning the Matson Building provide an interesting profile of the interrelationship of the front office to the architectural department and the pottery to the architect. In one memo, he

asked the Lincoln modelers to press out six different ornamental sections with six different shades of blue for the benefit of Bliss. As a usual practice, the department sent photographs of models to the architect for approval, but occasionally pictures did not suffice. Bliss apparently informed McBean that he did not want to take a chance of approving the cartouche carrying the client's symbol from a photograph. Instead, he planned to travel to Lincoln to inspect the model itself. However, McBean told the modeling department that next time it would help the architect if they supplied a side view along with the customary frontal shot. "Otherwise," he wrote, "an architect is asked to approve a model with very little definite information."

Bliss & Faville followed the romance of the sea theme throughout, especially when it came to the entranceway and base. No opportunity was overlooked, as even the volutes of the Ionic columns simulated coiled rope. *Shapes of Clay,* however, provided the best description of the entranceway:

The central ornament of the Market-street facade is a cartouche surmounted by a Viking ship with bellying sail, reminding the passer-by that Captain Matson, who created this great navigation company, was of Norse blood. The one touch of realism is found in the little panes showing actual steamships of the Matson fleet. The other elements of the ornament are symbolical — rope moldings and anchors, the trident of Neptune, the dolphin with its rich mythological allusiveness, the cockle-shell and the starfish.

Judging by the results, Lincoln draftsmen and modelers enjoyed expressing the imagination of Bliss and Faville through their medium. The ornamentation did not end with the entrance or base. A frieze of dolphins and tridents topped the main nine-story rusticated shaft; the heads of the massive Florentine windows of the upper stories featured starfish, and the cornice carried a series of large sea-shells. The entire structure was finished off with a two-story tower and an enamel and polychromed belvedere.

In a rare instance of recognition, Walter D. Bliss offered the following praise for his terra cotta contractor:

The particular use of terra-cotta that is illustrated in the Matson Building is peculiar to America. It was made possible when Gladding, McBean & Co. gave us these terra-cotta pieces, which are so much larger and straighter than any previously manufactured.

While work was winding down in 1923 on the Matson Building and several other local projects, the terra cotta works was awarded another contract for a monumental office building. Following World War I, Standard Oil's extraordinary growth required a larger and grander headquarters. After acquiring a choice site at the southwest corner of Sansome and Bush Streets, the giant company hired George W. Kelham as their architect. In concept, Kelham planned an L-shaped steel frame building twenty-two stories in height inspired in part by the then popular motif of the Italian Renaissance palaces.

From the viewpoint of the architect and his contractor, one of the primary problems for such a massive structure was the exterior color. Kelham selected California granite to clothe the three-story base and terra cotta for the shaft and attic. But to bring harmony to the whole, Kelham needed the terra cotta to match the gray tone of the base. The architect presented this challenge to the ceramic chemists in Lincoln and, after a year of experimentation in the laboratory and kiln, they discovered a satisfactory solution. Named "Granitex", the new terra cotta perfectly matched the color and texture of the stone base. To achieve the black speckled effect of granite, workers applied the glaze by means of "sputterers," a special spraying apparatus. At the same time, the staff in Lincoln developed a granite-like brick for the facing of the interior court. Hailed as a great advance in terra cotta practice, the ability of Granitex to mimic the natural stone of the Standard Oil Building earned Gladding, McBean the applause of the architectural community. It was a product that served them well in the near future as architects for buildings in Sacramento, Fresno and San Diego chose Granitex based on the success of the oil company's gleaming tower.

The pottery also supplied this industrial palace with tons of gray-toned terra cotta ornamentation for the upper stories. Kelham topped the eighteenth story with an opulent intermediate cornice accentuated with Florentine brackets. To give sufficient lighting for the storage room on the nineteenth floor, the pottery manufactured special perforated panels located between the brackets. Above the cornice rose a set back of another three stories punctuated with additional terra cotta brackets, panels, cartouches, capitals and rosettes. Kelham crowned the whole with a Gladding, McBean Cordova tile roof.

In a not too immodest turn of phrase, Edward F. O'Day in *Shapes of Clay* enthusiastically wrote of this giant building: "Viewed from the eucalyptus slope of Telegraph Hill, the Standard Oil Building presents an arresting facade of gray terra-cotta that adds new meaning to the poet's description of San Francisco as the 'cool gray city of love.'"

With the initial success of Granitex, more shafts of gray terra cotta followed. Adjacent to the Matson Building soared Bakewell and Brown's Pacific Gas and Electric Building. Erected in 1925, it too was clothed with Gladding, McBean Granitex and like other structures of the era followed a quasi-Italian Renaissance design.

In choosing Granitex, Bakewell and Brown offered eloquent testimony to the effectiveness of the new terra cotta product and the technique of rustication:

The treatment of the terra-cotta wall surface in rusticated courses serve two very useful purposes, one practical and one aesthetic. Large blocks of terra-cotta have a tendency to warp and twist in the process of making. The small grooves of the rustication break up the continuity of the surface, and the wavy appearance that would be apparent if the wall were absolutely of one surface is lost. These small grooves form continuous lines entirely around the building, carrying from one side of each window or opening to the other, and are of great assistance in tying the masses together. . . . In order to make the ornament, the fourteenth-story arcade, and other architectural detail appear to the best advantage, the use of a light-colored material was advisable. The most delicate ornament shows clearly, every line is revealed distinctly, and each shadow imparts its full impression on the light granite-gray color chosen.

The architectural ornamentation provided one of the most striking features of this 260-foot high structure. Sculptor Edgar Walter of San Francisco was commissioned to produce the models which the Lincoln staff transformed into glazed terra cotta. Walter chose themes symbolic of California and the corporation. For the arched niche of the entrance way, he modeled the head and paws of a California grizzly surrounded by fruit swags. Immediately above this scene, Walter flanked the name panel with two heroic figures symbolic of the utility's work force and other symbols of hydro-electricity. Bakewell and Brown complemented the entrance with a series of arched window openings. To accent these windows, Walter produced as the keystones the heads of the High Sierra bighorn sheep.

Following a now well-established formula for monumental buildings, Bakewell and Brown concluded the exterior with a series of ornamental terra cotta devices. The most striking feature consisted of a fourteenth-story arcade floor with oversized arched windows framed by graceful Doric columns. As O'Day enthusiastically described in the company magazine: "The crowning motive of the structure seems to burst through the business-like restraint of the shaft below, flowering out in column and entablature, obelisk, and pinnacle, all expressed in the plastic freedom of terra-cotta." To add further to the architectural drama, artificial lighting produced a spectacular nighttime effect when played off against the rusticated surface, Doric columns, and pinnacles.

In 1924, Gladding, McBean bid to manufacture terra cotta for one of America's finest skyscrapers, the Pacific Telephone and Telegraph Company Building. Located on New Montgomery Street and designed by the well-known firm of Miller, Pflueger and Cantin, it was at the time the largest corporate office building in the far West. The inspiration for the twenty-six story skyscraper came from Eliel Saarinen's Chicago Tribune Tower Competition. Today, the tower is recognized as one of the better early examples of Zigzag Moderne.

The Pacific Telephone Building promised to tax the resources of Gladding, McBean. Writing in February 1924, Atholl McBean informed the Lincoln staff that the drafting would be done in San Francisco and that by the time the contract was closed the drafting department would have finished the work on the Standard Oil and Pacific Gas & Electric projects. Atholl asked: "Could you take these buildings over and finish them at Lincoln so that we could clear the boards in the San Francisco drafting room? You might also have to take the College of the Pacific . . . I think by working a little overtime you might be able to complete . . . ." At this point, the hard driving company president listed four other projects.

The pottery had contracted for one of its largest jobs. The job order form in the project file included a standard section entitled "Extent of Terra Cotta." Simple as this statement may have been, it accurately described the extent to which the architects employed their product. It read: "From tip of granite base to coping, all terra cotta on New Montgomery, Minna, and Natoma Street frontages, and return on Minna Street over Gladding, McBean & Co. warehouse. Entire tower is terra cotta." Lincoln sent its first shipment of a 3,200 ton total on August 1, 1924, and made its final shipment on November 15.

The most striking feature of the building's concept was its surface design, and for this terra cotta played a dominant role. The architects unified the entire F-shaped building by the use of speckled terra cotta (Granitex) made to match gray granite. For ornamentation the pottery produced a number of notable features. Over the main entrance, Pio Tognelli created a polychrome bell in blue with white letters. A band of sconce-like stems or engaged columns were repeated between the sill and head of each window of the third and fourth floor. To add symmetry to this huge structure, the architects repeated this ornamentation on the fourteenth, eighteenth, and the nineteenth floor. While most of the facade was marked by simple dignity of Granitex, the architects utilized a floral motif to conclude many of the piers. As the building reached its conclusion or started another setback, the architects changed the stem-like sconce feature to where they unfolded in front of windows as double buds or opened out as triple finials of a giant Gothic gable, lotiform mushroom-headed caps and fleur-de-lisian. All these embellishments were produced by DeGolyer's staff in Lincoln.

The best, however, was reserved for the "glorified penthouse." As described by B. J. S. Cahill in *The Architect and Engineer* (December, 1925): "In design it repeats the motives of the rest of the building except that the eight finials over the four pairs of windows unfold to form a splendid perch for eight colossal eagles, standing twelve feet from beak to talon, scanning the world beneath in all directions and lording it over everything."

Before the decade closed, the kilns in Lincoln produced burnt clay for several other massive San Francisco projects. The Gothic-style Russ Building, rising thirty stories above Montgomery Street, was clothed in a record 3700 tons of specially manufactured rustic-surfaced "Pulsichrome" terra cotta. For the Hunter-Dulin Building a few blocks away, the factory provided buff Granitex facing and the tile for its striking Chateau roof. Of particular note are the terra cotta figures of the four seasons just below the roof line, the belt course decorated with bulls' heads and birds, second-story roundels, and the exquisite entrance. Off Union Square, for the Gothic style O'Connor-Moffatt Department Store (now Macy's) the pottery manufactured 401 tons of Granitex. Up on Nob Hill, architects made liberal use of Gladding, McBean products for the Mark Hopkins Hotel and the Huntington, Brocklebank and Cathedral apartment buildings.

While the pottery had left its mark on the financial district and Nob Hill, its kilns also produced work for scores of public and private structures throughout the city. The War Memorial Opera House and War Memorial Veterans Building in the civic center were clothed in terra cotta. Up on Mount Parnassus, several buildings for the Affiliated Colleges (later U.C. Medical School) featured terra cotta. Tucked away in the city's many neighborhoods were such striking edifices as the Gothic St. Dominic's Church and Romanesque St. Brigid's Church; the Della Robbia-style polychrome entrance for Children's Hospital; elegant branches of the public library, and elaborately ornamented schools including the Raphael Weill School, Mission High School and Alvarado School. For the latter two, the pottery manufactured spectacular facades of unglazed terra cotta inspired by Mexican church architecture.

In the 1930s, the use of architectural terra cotta in San Francisco declined dramatically. The Great Depression and a shift in style from elaborate Beaux Arts and Art Deco to Streamline Moderne brought this golden era to a close. As architectural historian Paul Gleye put it, the new generation wanted to inject into their buildings a feeling of efficiency with rounded corners, horizontal lines and clean surfaces. To be sure, Gladding, McBean and its competitors continued to produce architectural terra cotta for buildings, but not on the same grand scale as before. Advertisements in the architectural magazines depicted once ornate buildings stripped of their ornamentation and simplified to reflect streamlined design concepts. Gargoyles, cartouches, grotesques, Corinthian capitals, egg and dart patterns, and elaborate brackets gave way to the stark functionality of ceramic veneer and reinforced concrete as exemplified in their Union Oil and Roos Brothers buildings. Nonetheless, the company that had manufactured terra cotta for over 900 San Francisco buildings could, with justification, boast that it had indeed shaped the skyline of the City by the Bay.

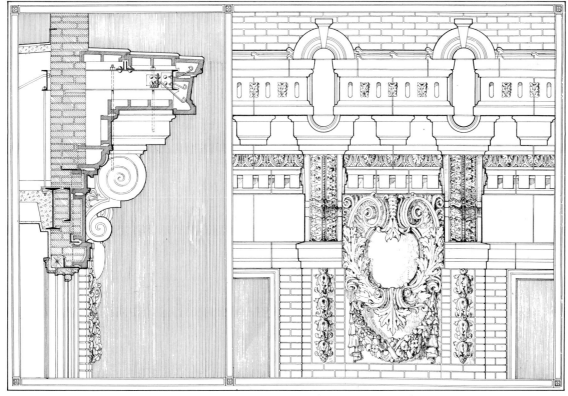

Terra Cotta Details, Cornice Construction, 1915

OAKLAND

Oakland and the East Bay, a region of civic and commercial optimism at the turn of the century, developed into lucrative territory for the architectural terra cotta trade. From the 1910s to the early 1930s, some of the most spectacular buildings of the Beaux Arts and Art Deco era graced the cities of Oakland, Berkeley, San Leandro, Richmond and Emeryville. Oakland, in particular, blossomed in terra cotta ranging from buildings clad in dignified gray and white to a jubilation of Art Deco color in the 1930s. The Oakland City Hall, Cathedral Building, Oakland Floral Depot, John Bruener Company, Paramount and Fox Theaters, I. Magnin's Store, and Singer Sewing Machine Shop, all in central Oakland, endure as some of the finest and most daring examples of architectural terra cotta in California.

Early in its history, Gladding, McBean put down roots in the East Bay. The Oakland City directory for 1877–78 lists the company at 1166–68 Broadway. An early panoramic photograph of the growing city by A. W. Wulzen shows the terra cotta works' Oakland outlet — a yard filled with clay products and a simple building dominated by two giant signs advertising its vitrified sewer pipe and chimney flumes and its 1875 founding date. Even then competition was keen, as Wulzen's panorama reveals that the pottery's chief rival N. Clark and Sons maintained a yard right next door. From these early beginnings on Broadway, Gladding, McBean expanded and by 1900 had opened a general sales office and warehouse on Twenty-second and Market

By the 1930s, the company had provided terra cotta for over 100 buildings in Oakland, making it the third largest concentration of Gladding, McBean buildings in California behind San Francisco and Los Angeles. This number does not reflect its traffic in more prosaic building materials such as pipe and tile. Early architectural projects included the gateway for St. Mary's Cemetery, Oakland Gas, Light, and Heat Company, the Telephone Building and the Bacon Land and Loan Company Building. Following architectural trends in other cities, the company received most of its contracts between 1910 and 1935. During the 1910s it completed twenty-two contracts; sixty-three in the 1920s and twenty-three in the 1930s. What these impressive figures do not reveal however, is that its competitors, Steiger, N. Clark and Sons, and others garnered contracts

of equal significance, including the Gothic-style Federal Realty Building (Cathedral Building), the flatiron First National Bank of Oakland, the Municipal Auditorium with its distinctive terra cotta niches, and the jewel-like Floral Depot.

Without doubt, the Oakland City Hall, with eighteen richly-ornamented stories, represented the most important Oakland job for Gladding, McBean. One of the city's most recognizable buildings and the first skyscraper city hall in the country, it was a robust statement of local pride. City fathers began planning the fifth Oakland city hall building in 1909 and, after passing a bond issue, raised over one million dollars to finance its construction. With a committee chaired by John Galen Howard, a noted proponent of the Beaux Arts school and chairman of the University of California Architecture Department, the city went out to bid. The prestigious New York firm of Palmer and Hornbostel won the architectural competition over twenty-four others. Palmer and Hornbostel designed a classic three-part steel-frame structure composed of a three-story base, transitional story, setback tower of nine stories, exaggerated cornice, and a penthouse crowned with a Baroque-style octagonal clock tower.

For this impressive 335-foot high building, the city also engaged twenty-seven sub-contractors and, on June 6, 1911, Gladding, McBean received the contract for the terra cotta work. The pottery supplied 960 tons of smooth matte enamel terra cotta for ornamentation that began with the first story and terminated at the top of the tower. Despite the building's tremendous height, the principal cladding consisted of Sierra granite supplied by Raymond Granite Company of San Francisco. The primary source of building stone in Northern California, their quarries were near the small Madera County town of Raymond.

Palmer and Hornbostel's Renaissance/Baroque design took full advantage of the plastic qualities of terra cotta. The firm contracted with M. R. Giusti of New York to create the models for all the ornamental work. Giusti then made quarter-scale models and shipped them to Lincoln where the finished pieces would be produced. Over the next three years, while Giusti created his models, the team in Lincoln received drawings from the architect; prepared shop drawings; sent photos of completed, full size models; made modifications after inspections by the architects; pressed, glazed and fired tons of cream colored terra cotta, and shipped it to the company's Oakland yard. Aside from routine delays and breakages, this massive job proceeded with little difficulty.

The end result was a symphony of shaped clay based on themes drawn from classical ages and California agriculture. Every level of the building featured terra cotta ornamentation. At the entrance were ornate light standards embellished with grapes, pinecones and acanthus. The three-story base supported a variety of terra cotta decorative pieces including a frieze of California grapes, olives, and figs that divided the first and second stories; complex pilaster caps; and muntins for the windows. Perched on the cornice were a pair of Roman eagles, those ubiquitous symbols of government.

Palmer and Hornbostel adorned the shaft with scenic spandrel panels. Over the shaft they placed an exaggerated cornice with dentils, modillions and a pierced rail. From the cornice sprang the great "wedding-cake" clock tower encrusted with Baroque ornamentation.

As the steel-frame skeleton for the city hall tower rose above Oakland, workmen also set terra cotta for the handsome Southern Pacific passenger station near 16th and Wood Streets. Like the city hall, this monumental structure reflected the "city beautiful" movement, the optimism that permeated local government and business. In previous decades, Gladding, McBean had been called upon to provide terra cotta for a half dozen depots but none as grand and stylish as this. Architectural critic Allan Temko summed up the significance of this Beaux Arts masterpiece:

Almost nothing is left in California to compare with the 16th Street Station. But as far as early 20th century classicism is concerned—the genuine article, not the diluted pastiches of the 1930s at Stockton or Sacramento—the Oakland Station is the only thing of its kind this side of Denver or the Pacific Northwest.

Designed by Jarvis Hunt of Chicago and built by James Stewart and Company of Denver, the station originally called for an exterior of artificial stone. The builders decided to switch to terra cotta, a material more compatible with the building's palatial design. Gladding, McBean got the job on June 7, 1911, to supply 350 tons of gray semi-glazed terra cotta. At first glance, the station appears as solid as a fortress, reflecting the power of the locomotive and of Southern Pacific. Stretching 270 feet across, the station's basic form is a large central block flanked by two side wings and a baggage building, all clad in terra cotta ashlar resting on a matching base of California granite. Three giant arches pierced the central block providing relief to the predominant square and rectangular shapes. Hunt embellished the depot with a simple yet dignified cornice, modillion blocks, balustrade, and panels. The granite-like ashlar blocks gave the depot a monumentality unobtainable by any other product except stone itself.

During the 1920s, Gladding, McBean shared in the tremendous growth of Oakland's downtown by providing terra cotta for a variety of commercial and civic enterprises. Most, however, consisted of smaller stores not requiring massive quantities of shaped clay. Noteworthy among its jobs were the trim for the distinctive tower of the Oakland Tribune Building; the Gothic Roos Atkins Building; S. H. Kress Building, and the Oakland Post Inquirer Building. The largest, the fifteen-story neo-Romanesque Central Savings Bank at Broadway and 14th Street, was designed by George Kelham and opened in 1926. The job to supply 842 tons of Granitex for the building presented some problems to Gladding, McBean. Correspondence reveals that P. O. Tognelli's models, created in San Francisco, did not survive the train ride to Lincoln and had to be returned to the artist's studio for repair and strengthening with wood and excelsior. To add to the company's woes, after the terra cotta pieces were finished, the foreman at the job site discovered that many of them had been improperly marked—they did not follow the markings specified in the shop drawings. For example, when the drawing called for a seven-inch wide piece, the actual item measured only five-inches. Further, many of the numbers on the terra cotta were not easily read as 9's looked like 4's and 3's looked liked 5's. To get around this problem, the workmen doing the actual installation simply interchanged pieces.

By the close of the decade, the Art Deco style that had gained favor among architects resulted in one of Oakland's finest examples, the Financial Center Building. Rising seventeen stories at the corner of 14th and Franklin Streets, and designed by Walter Reed and William H. Corlett, it represented an important addition to the skyline as well as being the downtown's only set-back or ziggurat-style building. In some respects, with its historical motifs, verticality of design, and set-back penthouse, the structure resembled San Francisco's telephone building. The 14th Street entrance carried a number of decorative features executed in terra cotta including interior piers depicting birds, grapes, flowers and foliage capped with rams-head corbels. Above the building's name panel rested a spandrel with a pair of eagles supporting a plaque depicting the city's symbol, a coast live oak. The architects employed ashlar for the piers and decorative spandrels featuring a geometric design for the base. A series of heraldic eagles clutching shields inscribed with the company's initials watch over each pier. For the main shaft, the architects used face brick. Terra cotta embellishment began again at the 13th story with decorative spandrels similar to the base and the main shaft concluded with a crenelated parapet. A stepped back ziggurat formed the caps for the merlons. The penthouse followed the same design. When completed in 1929, the tower won praise by the local press as a highly visible symbol of Oakland's vigorous financial district.

The early 1930s saw the creation of two of the company's most illustrious Art Deco projects, the John Bruener Department Store and Paramount Theater. Located on Broadway between Hobart and 22nd Streets and designed by Albert F. Roller, Bruener's massive cube-shaped emporium represented one of the finest early uses of machine-made ceramic veneer, which had come into vogue during the Depression. Cognizant that architects had grown weary of historical themes and heavy ornamentation and had turned to sleek streamline and simple configurations, Gladding, McBean was quick to advertise their low-cost ceramic veneer. The company referred to the veneer used on the Bruener Building as "Machine Made Terra Cotta." As noted in 1937 by the company:

Architects had long felt the need for a thin, lightweight ceramic veneer which would be economically practical as a building facade. Craftsmen wrestled with this problem for years in an effort to create a product which would meet the company's high standards of quality. At last, by de-airing the clay and dry-finishing the unburned material, a product was created which satisfied architects' requirements for size, weight, texture and color. The result is a ceramic which is both practical and attrac-

tive, and which gives promise of revolutionizing certain concepts and methods of building in the interest of both economy and design.

Extruded ceramic veneer offered many of the same advantages as traditional hollow terra cotta blocks, but was one-fifth lighter, cheaper to produce, offered an unlimited color palette and variety of texture, could be conveniently cleaned with soap and water, and was appropriate for current architectural styles. Ribbed on the back like tile, ceramic veneer was easily installed through a system of metal ties anchored to the building. This machine-made product could be produced in slabs with a maximum face size of $2'6'' \times 4'3''$ and a thickness of $1\frac{5}{8}''$. As Virginia Ferriday pointed out in her Portland study, it did have one major drawback: "As an extruded product, its decoration was limited to designs with all lines parallel to the extrusion axis." Thus decorations appeared as if in relief. Architects used the facing not only for new construction but also for modernizing older Beaux Arts or classical style structures. As defined by a 1936 company catalog:

[Ceramic veneer] is a new form of terra cotta, extruded by machinery through dies, under enormous pressure. It is made in hollow form, and being of a perfectly balanced symmetrical section, any tendency to warp is eliminated. Tiles are partly cut through the beds and after burning, cut portions are knocked out to provide openings for grout and for anchors. This type of ceramic veneer is suitable for plain ashlar only, where a large quantity of material of one width is required.

Gladding, McBean continued to manufacture hand-made veneer for decorative devices such as caps, inserts and grilles. The million-dollar John Bruener Store incorporated hand-made as well as machine-made ceramic. Originally, the building was finished with concrete. A memo from the San Francisco office dated February 2, 1931, indicated that the pottery had closed the contract with P. J. Walker Company (the builder) and agreed to furnish 101 tons of hand-made terra cotta and 23,000 square feet of machine extruded ashlar. Roller selected a bright, sea green glaze described by Gladding, McBean as "Celadon Green Terra Cotta." In referring to the store's sleek exterior, architectural critic Frederick Jones observed:

In the lines, masses, detail and color of the structure, the architect, Albert F. Roller, was careful to achieve sound and well coordinated design and to avoid sensational and bizarre effects. Thus, while the building is thoroughly modern, it is one that will always have good style, distinction and dignity.

Despite the severity of its facade, the architect's design did allow for some hand-made ornamentation typical of that restrained era. The Broadway entrance featured an allegorical bas-relief, symbolic of John Bruener's career in furniture making, depicting two muscular bare chested craftsmen applying the finishing touches to a throne-like chair. For the 21st Street entrance, Roller designed another bas-relief with a high-backed chair and bench with a background of sun rays flanked by a geometric design. Below both entrances were incised ashlar blocks carrying the company name and founding date. For the third-story belt course and eighth-story parapets, Gladding, McBean manufactured veneer incised with an abstract floral design.

Only a block away from Bruener's emporium rose another monument to the Art Deco era, the celebrated Paramount Theater. Designed by James R. Miller and Timothy Pflueger of San Francisco's Telephone Building and Medical-Dental Building fame, and with George Wagner as general contractor, this movie palace was erected during the ravages of the Depression. Ground breaking was December 11, 1930 and the opening a year later.

In designing the facade for this or any theater, Miller and Pflueger's challenge was to capture the public's attention with something utterly new, arresting and unforgettable. Without doubt, the architects succeeded in that endeavor; and as one observer wrote, "No passer-by could fail to recognize the function of this building." For the 50-foot wide, 100-foot high Broadway facade, the architects conceived what has been termed a gigantic billboard for the performing arts. It consists of a huge projecting aluminum sign that splits two 20 by 100-foot panels carrying a mosaic of glazed tile, framed by piers in deep, oxblood red tile. Manufactured by Gladding, McBean's tile specialists, the bold colors of the mosaic, when combined with the neon sign, created an extraordinarily clever and effective advertisement. This multi-colored mosaic, as described by B. J. S. Cahill in *The Architect and Engineer,* depicts:

two vast figures of a man and a woman, draped in embroidered folds of an Ionian chiton down to their feet, with their heads in a field of stars and stripes. These figures have their arms folded and from their fingers hang a dozen strings which work the puppets and marionettes of the plays and the circuses, the spectacles and exhibitions which make up the subjects of popular entertainment from ancient to modern times.

Despite the spectacular nature of this mosaic for the facade, little written evidence survives concerning its creation and the use of tile. It is recorded, however, that Gerald Fitzgerald, an artist in Miller and Pflueger's office, created the original cartoons that eventually gave life to the thousands of tiles that made up the double murals. Gladding, McBean, of course, used this achievement in their advertisements for architectural magazines and included the following summary of their work:

The two panels, covering the entire front of the building, are a great mosaic of glazed tile. The piers flanking the mosaic are likewise of glazed tile. They and the body of the large figures which hold the puppet strings representing theatrical characterizations are deep red. The background surrounding the figures is of gold tile, as are also the puppet strings and details of the figures themselves. In the smaller figures suspended by the puppet strings, color of a higher pitch of warmth and coolness have been introduced, running into bright vermillion and soft blues and greens, with other colors in a variety of shades.

The employment of machine-made ceramic veneer for Bruener's and the mosaic tile for the Paramount gained wide notice for Gladding, McBean and demonstrated its adaptability, if not contribution, to new architectural trends. The era of the streamline moderne ushered in new product lines that helped sustain the architectural department through the darkest days of the Great Depression.

Southern Pacific Station, Oakland, 1914

SACRAMENTO AND THE VALLEY

California's central valley proved to be fertile ground for Gladding, McBean salesmen. The pottery produced architectural terra cotta for scores of schools, court houses, banks, fraternal halls, utility company facilities, swimming pools, homes and business blocks from Chico to Bakersfield. While not receiving the general acclaim of structures like the Hobart Building in San Francisco or the Los Angeles City Hall, buildings in these smaller cities and towns included fine examples of Beaux Arts, Renaissance Revival and Art Moderne creations. Buildings like the Yolo County Courthouse in Woodland, the California State Life Insurance Building in Sacramento, Pacific Southwest Trust and Savings Bank in Fresno, and the buildings of the College of the Pacific in Stockton survive today as some of the finest architectural jewels in the Valley.

During the first quarter of the twentieth century, the architecture of these interior valley towns blossomed. William Wade in his descriptive article on "The Architecture of Small Cities" in the June 1920 issue of *The Architect and Engineer* observed how the growth of the interior cities coincided with an improved style of building. He wrote:

It seems that the day has passed when the visitor to an interior town or city is destined to look upon ramshackle affairs that never enjoyed so much as a resemblance of good architecture . . . It is only recently that our smaller cities have awakened to an appreciation of beautiful, substantial buildings. Competent men are now paid to design something worthwhile.

Wade continued his essay with a report on major new buildings found in the river city of Sacramento and pointed out "that Sacramento has more new buildings of a substantial type, population considered, than any other city in California." Interestingly, every building that he described or highlighted with photographs featured terra cotta. The same innovations in engineering and design that made possible the advent of giant skyscrapers in the large urban centers also influenced the architecture of the interior town. Generally, these innovations consisted of steel frame construction, reinforced concrete, the vogue of Beaux Arts classicism and Art Moderne architectural styles, and a heavy reliance on light-weight, economical, fire-resistant terra cotta products.

During this era of growth, the soft colors of terra cotta began to dominate the capital city. Edward F. O'Day devoted a special issue of *Shapes of Clay* to the phenomenal flowering of Sacramento and, of course, the role terra cotta and Gladding, McBean played in shaping its skyline. Despite the obvious self-serving nature of his journalism, O'Day nonetheless echoed the sentiments expressed earlier by William Wade:

Having found itself a city, Sacramento began a few years ago to build like a city. The transformation from a mining town into an agricultural and a manufacturing center had left it singularly drab and unattractive. Architects began to plead with their clients to open the door to beauty. . . . There followed an awakening to the uses of beauty in commercial architecture, and within the last few years so many beautiful buildings have been reared that it is like a city transformed. The skyline of Sacramento today is a metropolitan skyline. The somnolent town of a few decades ago, drowsing under the kindly Californian sun, is now a business-like and bustling modern city.

O'Day attributed this transformation of Sacramento to the development of several fine architects in the community, a growing appreciation by the owners and investors in architecture as an art form and community asset, and an awareness of architecture in larger cities. In short, Sacramento became beauty-conscious.

Despite having its primary works only 25 miles away, Gladding, McBean by no means dominated the Sacramento terra cotta competition. Steiger Terra Cotta and Pottery Works and N. Clark and Sons won many of the most important contracts for pre-1920s projects including the seven-story Capital National Bank Building, Masonic Temple and the city's best Beaux Arts structure, the City Hall. In fact, the Lincoln job order book listed fewer than fifty buildings in Sacramento between 1890 and 1930. This contrasted sharply with the hundreds listed for San Francisco and Los Angeles.

Nevertheless, the Lincoln pottery did secure contracts for several noteworthy buildings. The first on record was the California State Bank in 1889. It was, however, during the late 1910s and 1920s that the pottery did most of its Sacramento work. Their projects including the Capitol Extension buildings, California State Life Insurance, Telephone Building, Elks Building, Native Sons Hall, and the prestigious Senator Hotel. To produce these as well as several smaller business and governmental buildings, the pottery collaborated with the city's leading architects including Dean and Dean, Rudolph A. Herold, and George C. Sellon.

The 1917 fire that put Steiger Terra Cotta and Pottery Works of San Francisco out of business turned out to be beneficial for Gladding, McBean. At the time, Steiger was in the midst of producing the modeling for the Sacramento Public Library. Perhaps at the request of the architect, Gladding, McBean stepped in to complete the job for this three-story building. Interoffice memoranda suggest that Atholl McBean ironed out a smooth transition with Walter E. Dennison (Steiger's President) and the modelers who were engaged in the project. The fire had destroyed the modeling for the entrance and no photographs existed of any of the models. But all was not lost. One of Steiger's modelers, a Mr. Gorsuch, sent Dennison all of the architect's full-sized detail drawings for the entrance modeling, and the models and molds for the first floor survived the fire. Atholl wrote DeGolyer approving his suggestion to employ one of the Steiger modelers to finish the job "even if we have to pay him an exorbitant salary."

With these negotiations out of the way, Gladding, McBean commenced work on the library building. Designed by Loring P. Rixford of San Francisco and prominently situated on Plaza Park, the Italian Renaissance structure had a facade that combined buff-colored face brick with gray-brown terra cotta. The pottery supplied terra cotta for the first story, spandrels, belt course, cornice and cheneu. The ornamentation featured an elaborate projecting entrance-way with a broken scroll pediment supported by twin columns. Appropriately, a book and lamp of knowledge framed by two cornucopia crowned the pediment. Two ornate lamp standards supported by bear paws flanked the main entrance. Other details included a series of twelve lion heads on the first floor, spandrels embellished with cartouches below the large arched windows of the second floor and an enriched Florentine cornice. All coalesced to give the structure a dignified look reminiscent of the great Italian centers of learning.

In 1923 and 1925, Atholl McBean won contracts for two jobs that, along with the State Capitol's dome, dominated the Sacramento skyline for decades. Both the California State Life Insurance and Elks Club buildings represented important achievements for the pottery in its struggle to win favor in Sacramento, and both received widespread attention in the architectural magazines of the day. Designed by George C. Sellon of Sacramento, the California

Life Insurance skyscraper rose fourteen stories above Plaza Park at 10th and J Streets. The French Renaissance Revival office tower featured a twelve-story shaft and a two-story setback capped with a striking Chateauesque copper mansard roof. On clear days, the insurance building could be seen for miles on the Sacramento plain.

The chief problem for Gladding, McBean on the project revolved around color selection rather than the usual concerns over modeling, deadlines, and chipped blocks. The owners apparently liked the Granitex used for the massive Standard Oil Building in San Francisco, but the architect wanted to combine this gray shade with a Pulsichrome (mottled color) finish. The Pulsichrome finish was obtained by spraying the terra cotta with a multiple nozzle apparatus through which separate glazes were applied to the surface in separate pulsations or squirts. Worrying over this and its potential impact on the company's reputation, Atholl sent DeGolyer the following message of concern in February, 1923:

We have not been very successful in securing business in Sacramento. I hope you will give very careful consideration to the selection of the color. This is too big a building to try out something new. If the building looks a sight when it is up, it will certainly not help us to secure future business.

A month later and still fretting over the final color decision, Atholl wrote his trusted aid another letter:

We are very much exercised regarding this selection, as we believe this combination will not make an attractive building. We hate to see the owners make such a serious mistake, one that will be there for all time . . . They should decide on all either all Pulsichrome or all Granitex.

Pulsichrome it was. When the project was finished, company advertisements expressed great satisfaction with the building and touted its use of "rough dragged Pulsichrome terra-cotta with tooled surface in a warm buff color." Decorative terra cotta was used for balconies, cartouches, panels and an enriched cornice. Reigning as the tallest office building north of the Oakland City Hall and south of Portland, the insurance building stood as a powerful advertisement for Gladding, McBean.

No doubt the successful completion of this lofty building played a part in winning the contract for the Elks Club

Building of Hemming and Starks. Soaring 226 feet above the corner of J and 12th Streets, this majestic combination of Classical and Renaissance styles featured a series of setbacks, red-tiled hipped roof and a thirty-foot copper lantern. Its height surpassed that of the recently completed California Life Insurance tower. In winning this contract Gladding, McBean overcame competition not only from other terra cotta firms but also from other types of building materials such as cast stone, concrete, brick and granite. Grassi and Company, a manufacturer of Travertite cast stone had submitted a competing bid for the Elks Building. When the Elks' building committee had opened bids on September 16, 1924, Grassi offered a price of $57,000 and Gladding, McBean, $65,000. While Grassi's bid was lower, the committee had expected Travertite to be one-half the price of terra cotta. At this point, Gladding, McBean, sensing a chance, began an intensive campaign to lobby the members of the building committee and the California State Life Insurance Company (the building's financier) concerning the advantages of terra cotta over the less expensive but inferior cast stone. All were interviewed and invited to Lincoln and, after a certain amount of persuasion, the Elks agreed on terra cotta.

Once the bidding wars ended, workers clad the facade in Cannon and Company's "Orange Pink Face Brick" and 330 tons of cream-colored architectural terra cotta. The architects made liberal use of stock quoins, brackets, medallions, pilasters and pediments. Anyone looking at the massive structure from below quickly focused on its primary decorative feature: a series of huge terra cotta urns that rested precariously on the parapets of each level.

In addition to these distinctive towers, Gladding, McBean received commissions for a number of prominent business emporiums in the city. W. P. Fuller and Company, with its wire-brush surface of red terra cotta; Hart's Restaurant with its rusticated piers of French gray; and the polychrome entrance to the Herman Davis store masterfully demonstrated the comeliness and versatility of terra cotta for typical storefront establishments. Smaller storefronts such as these, while not monumental in character, added richness to a city whose architectural senses were, as O'Day observed, awakening.

On June 2, 1924, the region's best known department store Weinstock-Lubin and Company celebrated the opening of its new flagship store on K and 12th Streets. According to local newspapers, architects Powers and Ahnden of San Francisco took as a model the famed Printemps department store in Paris. The architects clothed the graceful three story building with a series of large windows, metal spandrels and "warm buff" pulsichrome terra cotta of "smooth texture." Twelve ornamental urns embellished the third story belt course. The main decorative attraction, however, consisted of an imposing recessed entrance arch that rose through all three floors. Composed entirely of terra cotta, the arch was one of the largest of its kind, measuring fifty feet in height, twenty-four feet in width and ten feet in depth. For the top of this arch, the modelers at Lincoln created a monumental cartouche. An article about the portal in the *Sacramento Bee* emphasized that the assembly of the pieces "was the most intricate part of the terra cotta work on the building."

Directly behind Weinstock's rose the city's most important hotel, the Senator. Built at the same time (1924) and proclaimed as "one of the most beautiful hotel buildings in the world," the Senator's exterior design was strongly influenced by the Farnese Palace in Florence. MacDonald and Couchot of San Francisco served as the architects. According to their scheme, the crowning glory of the luxury hotel was a 165-foot long Florentine portico that overlooked Capitol Park and the Capitol Building. A reporter wrote on opening day, "All of the dignity, massiveness and artistically beautiful work of the Italian Renaissance was worked into the exterior of the building." To enliven this palatial portico, the architects selected from the Lincoln pottery a "beautiful peach glow" Pulsichrome finish. The upper stories consisted primarily of reinforced concrete painted to match. The glazed terra cotta, however, set the pace and gave the hotel "the appearance of a palace of smooth worked marble in the Italian pink stone."

While all these commercial establishments were underway, Gladding, McBean contracted with the State of California to produce terra cotta for its largest building project in decades, the Capitol Extension group, located directly across the street from the Capitol. The state planned these twin buildings to house the State Library, Supreme Court and a number of other agencies. After considerable competition, the noted San Francisco firm of Weeks and Day received the architectural contract for this prestigious job.

Weeks and Day designed for the Greco-Roman Library-Courts and Office Building an impressive second story portico, and Edward Field Sanford received the commission to fill the huge pediments with allegorical sculptures symbolic of California's growth. McGilvray-Raymond Granite Company installed California granite for the stairway, first floor, piers, selected columns, and the second story belt course. To best complement the natural stone, the architects selected Granitex similar to that in the Standard Oil Building in San Francisco, and in March 1922, Gladding, McBean began production of the terra cotta. Because they stood alone without close neighbors, each five-story building was clad on all four sides with Granitex ashlar. As well, the Lincoln modelers produced a series of polychrome starbursts for the portico ceilings and the acroterion (ornaments) for the pediment roofs.

Coordinating the setting of the terra cotta with the installation of the granite caused some problems and delays. The granite company chipped or broke several pieces of terra cotta when one of its derricks fell on the roof of the Office Building during the installation of the granite for the pediments of both buildings.

Completion of the Capitol Extension buildings naturally drew attention from architectural circles, and the twin buildings received considerable praise from the press and critics for effectively framing the Capitol. However, Gladding, McBean and Company came under fire from state officials and Weeks and Day for not matching the color of the granite and, consequently, ruining the proportions of both buildings. While Gladding, McBean promoted the ability of their glazes to simulate granite, this project seemed to prove the difficulty of creating a perfect match. Atholl, in a communique to Lincoln on June 4, 1925, reproduced a letter he had received from the architects:

There is [only] a small percentage of terra cotta that matches the granite. The great field of terra cotta is very much darker and there are some pieces as dark as slate. One would have thought after the experience you had with the American National Bank and the Standard Oil Building you would not have repeated your mistake in these buildings. The building Committee, State Architect and ourselves were assured that you could match terra cotta. On that assurance on your part we based our recommendation that terra cotta be used in place of imitation stone. If

we had known the results would be as disastrous as they are, terra cotta would have been used without our consent.

The unfortunate result is that due to the dark color of the terra cotta the entire proportions of the building are changed. The dark frieze and attick [sic] become entirely too heavy to be supported by the delicate light columns, pilasters, etc., due entirely to the difference in color.

That summer the chemists in Lincoln worked feverishly to rectify the color problem. Giving the blocks an acid bath failed and ordinary oil paint did not work. Instead, the pottery experimented with applying Atlas white wet cement with a paint brush to dampened blocks. "The question in our minds," wrote Atholl, "is will this cement come off in a few years." Unfortunately, the pottery did not document its final solution (if any) but, judging by present day appearances, a trained eye will spot a smattering of darker terra cotta blocks. In any event, the weathering of the buildings and passage of time appear to have sufficiently masked any obvious differences between granite and Granitex.

Two other significant civic projects involving the Lincoln works adorned downtown: the Memorial Auditorium and Post Office Building. In commissioning the construction of the Auditorium, city officials wanted a building that would take its place among the monumental structures of the nation and would also reflect building materials indigenous to the valley. As explained by City Architect James C. Deon, "Wherever the development of civilization has taken place in great river valleys, there has arisen an architecture of brick made from alluvial deposits." Consequently, the city chose to clad the auditorium in materials produced by local kilns. Canon and Company of Sacramento furnished the brick as the primary material for the facade, and Lincoln manufactured a rough drag, buff-colored terra cotta for the trim and ornamentation.

The Auditorium provides a good example of how architects made use of terra cotta as a secondary material. Designed by the renowned architectural firm of James S. Dean, G. A. Lansburgh and Arthur Brown, the huge building was unique in the region because its motif was Byzantine rather the usual Renaissance or Mission Revival style. By choosing a Byzantine look as developed in northern Italy in the fifth and sixth centuries, the architects incorporated several details that only a material with the plasticity of terra cotta could produce. The main entrance consisted of a huge portico faced in ashlar with deep carved letters, an enriched cornice, and a series of six medallions over the doors. Six towering stone columns with a decorative entablature supported the whole. Each column was crowned with an intricate terra cotta basket capital. Completed in February 1927, the Memorial Auditorium won immediate approval and caused one congratulatory contractor to write: "Sacramento's City Council has erected in the new Memorial Auditorium a living monument whose colorful charm and stately dignity will be enhanced — not dimmed — by the passing years."

During this era of monumental buildings based on neoclassical and Renaissance revival styles, Gladding, McBean created the facades for at least thirty-three post offices from Honolulu, Hawaii, to Sitka, Alaska, to Phoenix, Arizona. Most were erected during the early 1930s and helped assuage some of the company's financial damage caused by the Great Depression. The Post Office Building constructed in Sacramento in 1933 ranks as one of Gladding, McBean's finest monumental government structures and their largest job in the river city.

As designed by Starks and Flanders of Sacramento, the plan called for a four story neo-Classical or Roman structure. Following a formula repeated scores of times across the county, the Post Office's facade consisted of a first story of granite. Thereafter, matching Granitex took over. En toto, Lincoln produced 863 tons of molded clay for three elevations. The rear consisted of matching face brick. Prominent features included a stately colonnade with Doric capitals, rusticated ashlar, decorative swag panels, detailed cornice, and a series of ten lion-heads. These snarling felines stare across the street at the terra cotta lions that adorn the Public Library.

Gladding, McBean and Company shaped clay for projects in dozens of small towns throughout California, and frequently, these were a community's most important structure such as a city hall, court house, library, high school, bank or public swimming pool. One of the finest civic projects employing terra cotta in California's interior was the Renaissance Revival Yolo County Courthouse in nearby Woodland.

For this project, the county commissioned architect William H. Weeks and contractor Robert Trost, both of San Francisco. In 1916 Gladding, McBean provided terra cotta that began with the granite base and terminated with the top of the second story parapet wall. Even though Lincoln was a short distance from Woodland, the pottery sent the finished product to the job site via Northern Electric Railroad through Sacramento.

As demonstrated by this job, the architects did not always have their minds made up about decorative details. Apparently Weeks wanted to have four statues above the main entrance. A memo from San Francisco to DeGolyer stated, "Mr. Weeks suggests you send plates or cuts suggestive of anything you have which could be used for these." Based on this vague instruction, P. O. Tognelli began creating models on a design of his own selection. A month later, San Francisco reported: "Mr. Tognelli submitted his sketch models to Mr. Weeks and found them to be just about what the latter had in mind." After Weeks approved front and side view photographs, Tognelli went into full production and created a series of two spear-carrying Roman soldiers and two comely ladies who now gaze down on all who enter this hall of justice.

The company's front office was acutely aware of the advertising value of such a monumental civic project. On an inspection trip, Atholl McBean wrote DeGolyer: "The terra cotta looked exceedingly well — nicely jointed, well fitted and well set. I believe this building will do more to help us get terra cotta specified for court houses than anything we have ever done." With this in mind, Atholl instructed DeGolyer to take a photographer to the building site. The completed Yolo County Courthouse pleased Weeks and no doubt contributed, as Atholl had predicted, to securing much additional work for similar civic edifices.

Naturally, the company town of Lincoln served as a showcase for Gladding, McBean, and its streets are lined with buildings of terra cotta blocks, brick, tile roofs, and ornamentation. The job order book lists nearly two dozen local projects for this "Clay City" including the private residence of Albert J. Gladding, two bank buildings, and several civic projects including the public library, high school, grammar school, and civic auditorium. Frequently, the pottery generously donated or sold materials at cost for local public buildings. To celebrate its fiftieth anniversary in 1925, the corporation pleased the people of Lincoln by donating a swimming pool in memory of Peter McGill

McBean, dedicated on May 23. The local newspaper proclaimed the event to be "The biggest Celebration in the History of Lincoln."

The growing inland port city of Stockton also produced its share of important terra cotta buildings. Perhaps Gladding, McBean's most significant job of enduring value was for the buildings of the College of the Pacific when it moved its campus to Stockton in 1924. To give it the ambiance of an Ivy League campus, the architects of David-Heller-Pearce Company designed the cluster of Gothic Revival buildings. R. W. Moller served as the general contractor, and he contracted with the pottery. According to the work order, Lincoln was required to manufacture 316 tons of smooth-glazed pulsichrome for the Science Building, Power House, Administration Building, Dining and Social Hall, Girls Dormitory, Auditorium and Tower, President's House and Boys Dormitory. Red common brick was to be used as the primary exterior material.

The architects originally planned to use cast cement for the trim and ornamentation. Moller, the contractor, did not agree and influenced the architects into making a change, saying that the buildings "would look like warehouses without terra cotta trim." The pottery's front office in San Francisco recorded in the usually terse job order sheet: "We have been awarded this contract on account of the superiority of terra cotta in place of cast cement."

After Lincoln received the architects' plans in March 1924, the modelers and kiln-masters began their work. Because time was of the essence, most of the production consisted of stock terra cotta. For example, for the Boys Dormitory, the instructions received in Lincoln stated:

Everything on the Boys dormitory will practically be stock; the entrances being taken from the other buildings. The Architects are using these molds with the idea of getting a quicker delivery . . . We would suggest that all of the molds for the College of the Pacific be segregated and kept indefinitely, as they will be used from time to time.

By the end of the year, the pottery had shipped most of the Pulsichrome via railroad to Stockton. The end result was a significantly enhanced campus. Pleased to be associated with this educational center, the pottery devoted its March 1927 *Shapes of Clay* to the campus and the effectiveness of terra cotta trim and ornament.

Further to the south in Fresno, the Lincoln staff manufactured terra cotta for two of that city's largest buildings, the ten-story San Joaquin Light and Power Building and the fifteen-story Pacific Southwest Trust and Saving Bank. R. F. Felchlin Company of Fresno designed both structures and was most familiar with the work and reputation of Gladding, McBean. The pottery manufactured the terra cotta for both buildings in 1923 and 1924 and, as borne out by company files, enjoyed a good working relationship with the architects.

Work began first on the power company's building, a monumental structure that would have looked at home in San Francisco's financial district. A short article in *The Architect and Engineer* indicated that Felchlin planned to take advantage of the properties of brick and terra cotta by use of lights to make it one of the central valley's most dramatic structures. According to the architectural firm, "Flood lights in colors are to give the brick and terra cotta facing a spectacular brilliancy, making it visible from points several miles from Fresno."

For this handsome Beaux Arts office building, the pottery produced smooth surface Granitex terra cotta that extended from the top of the granite base and terminated below the crown mold to the attic cornice. A "Library Gray" face brick was also supplied for the facade. Raymond Shaw, Felchlin's associate, provided detailed drawings and inspected the modeling up to the top of the third floor. Thereafter, he relied on photographs sent from Lincoln.

Initially, however, there were misunderstandings between architect and contractor. A letter from Felchlin in May 1923 complained that the pottery was forty-five days late in making its delivery. "I do not know," wrote one of the architects, "how we can store 50,000 brick at the building, as we will need the entire first floor to sort the Terra Cotta." Atholl, however, offered the following rejoinder: "You have probably forgotten you did not furnish us with the drawings at the time we signed the contract." To correct any misunderstandings, Atholl promised he would do everything to hurry the job along and added: "If you see to it that we get the order for the roof tile for this building we will accept your apologies."

Throughout the remainder of that year and into 1924, the pottery's kilns turned out the thousands of individual pieces for the facade of this mammoth building. Renaissance revival in style, the power company's headquarters featured an elaborate base, belt course, a two story colonnade beginning with the eighth floor, penthouse or attic and a tile mansard roof. Obviously pleased with the end results, R. F. Felchlin wrote Atholl on October 9, 1924 one of the most complimentary letters received from an architect:

With reference to the modeling, jointing and general workmanship, I believe this work to at least equal the best in terra cotta which has come under my notice.

I want to make particular reference to the question of texture and color. I believe your company deserves the appreciation of the profession because of your efforts in developing special finishes which are new and distinctive in the matter of color and texture. In this connection I believe the terra cotta surpasses any that I know of.

While work progressed on this building, the Pacific Gas and Electric Building in San Francisco and the Capitol Extension buildings in Sacramento, the Lincoln works began manufacturing terra cotta for the spectacular Pacific Southwest Trust and Savings Bank. Rising fifteen stories and crowned with a revolving light, the 260-foot Beaux Arts tower was intended to symbolize the agricultural prosperity of Fresno County and the valley. When completed, it stood as the region's tallest building until the 1960s. Gladding, McBean's contribution was 492 tons of Granitex that extended from the base to the top of finials and vases over the parapet at the fifteenth floor. The pottery apparently won the contract not only because of its work on the power company building but also because of the Granitex finish that it had developed for the Standard Oil Building in San Francisco. A memo dated August 29, 1923 revealed:

We have received this contract, getting a preference over two of our competitors, on account of our being able to make delivery and furnish the special finish terra cotta which the owners have taken a fancy to; this color being the same as furnished for the San Joaquin Light & Power Building, which is certainly a credit to us.

The pottery's file on this project specified the typical order in which they manufactured terra cotta for a tall building. Because the work on the first, mezzanine and second story required more modeling, the executive office assigned this more complex job to the Lincoln drafting room. The San Francisco draftsmen completed the rest of the building. Also, because of great amount of modeling for the first two floors, the setting of the terra cotta actually began with the intermediate stories and not the bottom. The pottery's executives often employed this strategy in order to speed up delivery and keep architects happy. Despite these plans, the pottery fell behind in production and this incurred the wrath of the supervising architect, Raymond R. Shaw. Writing the crew directly in Lincoln, he reminded them how late they were with the "Power Co." job and warned that continued delay would result in a colossal loss.

Notwithstanding Shaw's warning, further delays did occur caused by corporate ego and a desire to establish a unique identity for the building. A letter from R. F. Felchlin in September 1924 to Atholl carried the following message:

A circumstance has arisen in connection with the eagles used on the building. It seems that the eagle which has always been symbolic of money and banking is not looked upon with favor by the Pacific Southwest Bank, owing to the fact that said bird has been grossly misplaced and now adorns the entrance and frieze of a certain bank in Los Angeles, known as the Bank of Italy. Therefore, it behooves us to omit wherever shown on our design this noble bird, and substitute in its place some beast of the field. We are now making some studies for entrances and are trying anything from roosters to bears.

For reasons not recorded, the owners again changed their minds and went back to the traditional eagle. A terse letter signed by Shaw with a photograph of an approved model of an eagle was received in Lincoln the following January.

Gladding, McBean and Company played a major role in sculpting Fresno's skyline, as it did with other cities. The city's first skyscraper, the Griffith-McKenzie Building (1914), Radin & Kamp department store (1925), six story Rowell Building (1912), Elks Building (1927), and Pacific Telephone and Telegraph Building (1925) were among the more prominent structures that featured Gladding, McBean terra cotta. Today, many of these survive as Fresno's most distinctive buildings.

LOS ANGELES AND SOUTHERN CALIFORNIA

Early in its history, Gladding, McBean and Company's architectural terra cotta found its way into the boom town of Los Angeles. A company catalog issued around the turn of the century, one of the earliest to feature architectural terra cotta, listed eight buildings in Los Angeles and two in neighboring Pasadena. Noteworthy examples of pre-1900 buildings included the fashionable residence of L. L. Bradbury designed by Samuel and Joseph C. Newsom, J. B. Lankershim's Main Street Building, and the Westminster Hotel.

According to architectural historians David Gebhard and Robert Winter in their invaluable *A Guide to Architecture in Los Angeles & Southern California,* Los Angeles and its environs have experienced three major building booms. The first, characterized by classical Beaux Arts and ten to twelve story business blocks, extended from 1905 to the early 1920s; the second, the Monumental Moderne, enjoyed its heyday in the late 1920s, and the third began in the 1960s and continues today. Of these three booms, the first two occurred when the medium of terra cotta had its greatest acceptance by architects and contractors.

Oswald Speir in an exuberant article on "The Development of Architectural Terra Cotta on the Pacific Coast" (*The Architect and Engineer,* September 1912) wrote:

And then from the south there looms in meteoric splendor the great city of Los Angeles, almost exotic in its sudden demand for merited recognition; and as she pushed her great buildings skyward we find them too, clothed in architectural terra cotta and the city glorious in her mantle of white and soft gray.

Speir, manager of the pottery's Los Angeles office, went on to write that the reason terra cotta enjoyed such popularity was the lack of local stone of satisfactory color and quality and, most importantly, the responsiveness of his trade to the demands of the architect and owner. The advent of the steel frame building and reinforced concrete meshed well with the products of California's kiln masters. Incidentally, in a sagacious bit of advertising, Gladding, McBean and Company furnished all the illustrations for Speir's article.

By the turn of the century, Los Angeles and its neighboring communities were growing in quantum leaps and successful entrepreneurs demanded buildings that not only demonstrated their financial prowess but also their city's claim to respectability. Beaux Arts classicism, then the architectural vogue nationwide, matched this desire. The Union Trust Building (also known as the Braly Block and later the Hibernian Building) at 408 Spring Street and the Herman W. Hellman Building at 354 South Spring led this early skyward push. Gladding, McBean furnished the ornamental terra cotta for both structures.

Rising twelve stories and designed by the prominent architect John Parkinson, the impressive Union Trust Building, called the city's first skyscraper, followed the classic Italian Renaissance palace formula of an ornate base, shaft, and elaborate attic decorated with terra cotta columns, cartouches, brackets, window pediments and exaggerated cornice guarded by a series of lion heads. Lincoln shipped the glazed terra cotta in the summer of 1903, and by May of the following year Parkinson gave permission to destroy the molds. On May 6, 1904, Atholl McBean relayed to DeGolyer a letter of jubilation: "Mr. Parkinson is very pleased with the new Southern California Savings Bank [the building's first floor occupants] and I think it is about the best piece of work we have ever done."

St. Louis architect Alfred F. Rosenheim, a vigorous proponent of steel framed construction, designed the neighboring Hellman Building. Proclaimed as the finest architectural monument in the city when it was completed in November 1904, the eight-story bank building featured a two story base of native gray granite and shaft of gray pressed brick trimmed with cream colored terra cotta.

Work on the Hellman Building so consumed Rosenheim that he moved to Los Angeles permanently. His next important assignment was the "Great" Hamburger Department Store (now the May Company), at the southwest corner of Eighth and Broadway. Its owners proudly stated that it would rank as the largest retail business building west of Chicago. The mammoth store rose five and a half stories and incorporated the latest architectural innovations. Apparently pleased with Gladding, McBean's work on the Hellman Building, Rosenheim selected the Lincoln pottery to provide the terra cotta. He selected cream white "lustrous" (enameled) terra cotta to clothe the building from the second story belt course to the top of the parapet wall. (In 1915 and again in 1923, Lincoln provided terra cotta for modification and expansion of the building.)

Los Angeles Theater, Los Angeles, 1931

Completion of the prestigious Hamburger Department store in 1906 established Gladding, McBean as one of the principal manufacturers of terra cotta for southern California. Following this success, the pottery in Lincoln shipped tons of fired clay southward for such important Beaux Arts era buildings as the Los Angeles Trust and Savings Bank, Kerckhoff Building, Van Nuys Building, Title Guarantee Building, Walter P. Story Building, Hollingsworth Building and Union Oil Company. As in San Francisco, the pottery worked with the leading architects of the region who included not only Rosenheim but also Parkinson and Bergstrom, and Morgan and Walls. Los Angeles' skyline was undergoing a rapid transformation into towers of gray, cream, and white terra cotta.

Several of these new buildings reflected not only the versatility of terra cotta but the artistic skill of the sculptor. In 1911, members entering the new Los Angeles Athletic Club were treated to an entrance way adorned with three graceful athletes fashioned out of terra cotta fired in Lincoln. These free-standing statues were flanked by two bas-relief medallions featuring sportsmen. All these figures were created for the club by Domingo Mora, a celebrated sculptor and father of Jo Mora. The opportunity to work with Mora must have been an inspirational boost for the staff in Lincoln. Spanish born and previously employed by the Perth Amboy Terra Cotta Company in New York, Mora was one of the first sculptors in the United States to execute statues, medallions, panels and bas-reliefs in terra cotta. The staff was so impressed by the work of the master that they preserved parts of the plaster casts of these figures in the modeling rooms at the factory.

Domingo Mora collaborated with Gladding, McBean on another interesting Los Angeles project in 1911 when the pottery won the contract for the New Orpheum Theater and Office Building (now the Palace Theater). The pottery produced 123 tons of terra cotta for this entertainment palace that had been designed by the renowned theater architect G. Albert Lansburgh of San Francisco. To embellish the facade and interpret the spirit of vaudeville, Mora executed four figure panels representing Music, Song, Comedy and Dance. These in turn were supported by glazed and polychrome cornices, spandrels, keys and friezes that included a wonderful array of bells, harps, grape clusters and mascarons (masks) as detailing.

While Mora's creations set the tone, terra cotta further enriched the building's lustre. To indicate to the public that this business building contained a theater, Lansburgh decided to introduce color into the facade. And it was this feature that not only challenged the staff at Lincoln but reaped the greatest reward. Oswald Speir wrote to J. B. DeGolyer in December 1910 concerning the polychrome used for Mora's figure panels:

The colored figure panels have arrived and technically they are the most beautiful pieces of Polychrome Architectural Terra Cotta we have ever seen. Unfortunately the colors have not been applied in some cases in accordance with the original models. The most glaring example is in the robes of the male figures, which in both cases were to have been Dark Green Matte (10163). In one case you have used Rockingham Yellow #1016f and in the other case Ivory tone.

We are doing some color experimenting on these figures which we have here and will work out the changes desired and send them to you indicated on a photograph.

Evidently, the use of polychrome for the facade attracted a great deal of attention from visiting architects and architectural critics. For example, Atholl McBean informed the Lincoln staff that the architects for the new Oakland City Hall were visiting from New York and hoped to stop by Lincoln, as they were considering a similar terra cotta treatment. This early use of polychrome foreshadowed the 1920s when architects made liberal use of it. William Cline in an article for *The Architect and Engineer* of September 1911 described the importance of the polychrome facade:

The facade is replete with color, but so beautifully harmonized that it satisfies the taste and leaves the spectator delighted with this new venture in polychrome designing. The Orpheum has the first colored facade to be erected in Los Angeles, and one of the first in the West. Its beautiful semi-glazed terra cotta is the first of its kind to be made in California and the most many colored yet produced in one burning, each new color formerly requiring a separate firing.

Gladding, McBean contracted to produce terra cotta for one other important theater building in downtown Los Angeles, the Pantages. The preeminent theater designer B. Marcus Priteca from Seattle served as the architect for Alexander Pantages' nine story building on Seventh and

Hill Streets. Earl Newcomb assisted as the resident architect. Its design called for terra cotta to be incorporated from the top of the granite base to the top of a Baroque style dome and for the creation of several ornamental devices.

Company correspondence on the Pantages project illustrates the problems and challenges encountered with a Los Angeles building designed in Seattle and faced with terra cotta manufactured in Lincoln. Speir acted as the local liaison. In June 1919 Atholl McBean entered into negotiations for the contract. Writing Lincoln, he informed them that Speir had sent up plans to begin work on the shop drawings. Speir also told McBean that there was little risk in starting the drawings before the contract had been signed as "we were the logical people to do the work." As work began, however, the pottery quickly ran into difficulties. Speir complained that the architect's drawings lacked completeness and "that we will make shop drawings to the best of our ability." Despite this problem, shop drawings for the cornice work for the second through eighth floor had been sent on for approval by summer's end. Lincoln's chief modeler P. O. Tognelli also expressed a need to meet with Priteca before proceeding further. By September, the company received news that Priteca himself would visit Lincoln to approve modeling and make final decisions on color.

At this point, criticism changed to words of mutual admiration as Priteca informed the drawing room and modeling staff that he appreciated their ability to capture the feeling, spirit and scale of his drawings. Tognelli was required to produce a complex ornamental cartouche above the box office for the Pantages. Writing to the Lincoln office, Speir summarized Priteca's opinion:

Mr. Priteca is very much pleased with the modeling of Mr. Tognelli's interpretation of his drawing, but fears that it is a little unrestful in the pose of the figures, a trifle too fine in detail and that the drapery over the figures is too thin and flexible. He does not wish the figures to appear as nudes or to be too suggestive of the contours of the figures.

For the classical figure of a young woman with a basket of flowers over head surrounded by musical instruments and fruit, Speir complimented Tognelli. But he added:

I am particularly delighted with the sharp, crisp treatment of the draperies, which, I think are most intelligently exaggerated to accept the enamel and still carry the proper feeling of the model-

ing. My only other point would be that Mr. Tognelli find a young woman with real California legs, which would mean a trifle more shapeliness than he has indicated.

Whether Tognelli found such a girl in Lincoln is not known, but work on the theater appeared to progress well. Photographs showing details of cornices, pilasters, pillar caps, cartouches, caryatids, panels, spandrels and huge sections on the great corner dome were sent on for approval. A November 24, 1919, memo from Speir informed the pottery that the roof of the building would be poured shortly and asked that they begin shipping the terra cotta. The contractors planned to set the front at a rate of one and a half stories per week. The chronic problem of damage during shipment was made potentially worse by the long rail trip from Lincoln to Los Angeles. But the first shipment arrived in good condition and, as revealed by another memo, a new packing material was the reason:

This rice straw which we are using for packing appears to be even more satisfactory than the old tule hay which we used for so many years. The rice straw is in just as good shape after the terra cotta is unloaded at the building as it was when it was first used, showing that it is not soft and easily broken, as is wheat straw.

Because of the fragile nature of terra cotta, potteries frequently devoted an entire department to the painstaking task of packing the final product. Nevertheless, careless truckmen and laborers sometimes chipped or broke beautiful and complex pieces. After the first story had been completed, Speir told the Lincoln staff how good it looked and gave them added incentive to speed up their production. Often intercompany memos complained about the performance of the architect or contractor, but in this case the opposite was true. Speir wrote:

May I say that these people have the nicest and friendliest feeling toward us and having nothing but compliments to offer on the way we have handled the job, i.e. they are friends of ours. It seems quite likely that Mr. Priteca may be awarded the commission for a very large building here, which will use a great deal of terra cotta. It is logical, therefore, to assume that we will do everything possible to assist our friend.

Completion of the Pantages Theater early in 1920 exemplified architectural terra cotta at its best. The theater's striking Baroque terra cotta dome, the exquisite figures created by Tognelli, and the pleasing overall effect of the terra cotta facade complemented the genius of Priteca. It seemed only fitting that a city that soon became known for its performing arts should build such wonderfully ostentatious facilities. The pottery also provided terra cotta for the famous Orpheum theaters in Kansas City and Salt Lake City and the Junior Orpheums and Loew's State Theaters in Los Angeles and San Francisco. All were designed either by Lansburgh or Priteca.

Among the finest examples of the malleability or "plasticity" of terra cotta which the manufacturers consistently boasted about, were the griffins and gargoyles for the ten-story Knickerbocker Building, built in 1913. Architects John C. Austin and William Pennell designed the Gothic-style skyscraper on South Olive Street and called for a variety of decorative mythological beasts. DeGolyer's artists in Lincoln went to work and soon sent photos of their models directly to the architects for approval.

As with all jobs, a unique number code was assigned to each piece. For example, the second-story griffin was numbered 1052BL5 (job order 1052, section number BL, mold number 5). This way the pottery could easily identify a damaged piece to be replaced. The following letter from Pennell concerns "1052BL5":

Front view of BL5: the left fore-leg is too heavy. Referring to right elevation of same, you will see that it has the proper contour while the front has been made too coarse and heavy, and I doubt if the muscle will twist across the bone as shown. The plain surfaces at the jaw and in the bill seem a little bit coarse. Raising the wings as suggested on the two side views of Griffin will take away the apparent extreme length of neck shown on the front. On the right elevation the wings should be raised as shown.

To assist the modelers, the architects frequently drew directly on the photograph or pasted over it with a sketch to highlight areas requiring change. In March 1913 Austin sent to Lincoln penciled-in photographs of one of the gargoyles with the accompanying verbal instructions:

Most of the modeling on the gargoyle is satisfactory; however, I would suggest that you give a greater slant to the eye-brows, and that the eyes be more deeply cut; also, that the horns be slightly elongated and that instead of slanting backward they slant towards the front. With these exceptions, the work is very satisfactory.

As Gladding, McBean grew and assets multiplied, the company began to swallow its smaller rivals. In 1922 the San Francisco office negotiated the takeover of Tropico Potteries, Inc. of Glendale and in 1924 the Los Angeles Pressed Brick Company.

Founded in 1904 and known earlier as the Pacific Art Tile Works, Tropico specialized in small faience and floor tile. With its acquisition for $500,000, Gladding, McBean made the wise decision of expanding the production of decorative tile. An organization of artists and technicians under the skillful leadership of J. B. Stanton perfected its architectural applications. Through the Tropico Plant, Gladding, McBean offered its exquisitely colored "Hermosa" tiles for use in public buildings, businesses, swimming pools, gas stations, bathrooms, and fireplaces. Eighty-five different colors and a variety of shapes and sizes were available. Fireproof and having an indestructible finish, Hermosa tile was used in more than one-third of the new homes of the Pacific Coast. Important jobs installed by Tropico included the decorative tile at the plush Agua Caliente resort, Hotel del Monte, Pasadena Civic Auditorium, Los Angeles City Hall, Calpet Petroleum stations, Pig N' Whistle restaurants, the bathroom of Buster Keaton, and the living room of movie producer Ernst Lubitsch. Further, Tropico's talented staff of artists also produced tile murals depicting historical scenes or symbolic themes for businesses and institutions.

The takeover of the Los Angeles Pressed Brick Company solidified the primacy of Gladding, McBean and Company as the largest terra cotta manufacturer in the West. Established in 1887 by Charles H. Frost, Los Angeles Pressed Brick Company flourished as the principal producer of face brick in the region and also supplied architectural terra cotta for buildings as far away as Idaho Falls. At the time of its merger with Gladding, McBean, Frost's business owned and operated four plants equipped with 31 kilns in Los Angeles (952 Date Street), Santa Monica (the former Sunset Brick and Tile Company), Point Richmond in Northern California, and Alberhill in Riverside County. A rich deposit about one mile from Alberhill supplied Frost's company with white and gray clay.

With the Tropico works and Los Angeles Pressed Brick Company (both still retained their names), the Southern Division of Gladding, McBean and Company secured a number of important local jobs in the 1920s. Prospective clients could visit its factory and show room near the Southern Pacific tracks on Los Feliz Boulevard in Glendale, or the permanent display on the roof top of the Pacific Finance Building at 621 Hope Street in downtown Los Angeles to view its pottery, tile, and terra cotta ornamentation. Among the prestigious jobs secured in the 1920s were the Biltmore Hotel, Bank of Italy Building, Fine Arts Building, Mercantile Arcade, Pacific Mutual Building, Roosevelt Building, Barker Brothers, United Artists Building, Los Angeles Theater, Beverly-Wilshire Apartment Building, and Title Insurance and Trust Company Building. Because of the thirteen-story height limit imposed in Los Angeles, however, none of these projects matched the terra cotta output required for the skyscrapers of San Francisco, Portland and Seattle. Because of Gladding, McBean's size and reputation, the major architectural firms of the area including Morgan and Walls and Morgan, Robert D. Farquhar, Curlett and Beelman, Walker and Eisen, Schultze and Weaver, and Austin, Parkinson and Martin selected the pottery for major jobs without solicitation of competitive bids.

One of the most notable landmarks to rise in downtown Los Angeles during the 1920s was the thirteen story Mercantile Arcade Building of Adolph Ramish. Patterned after London's Burlington Arcade, this great glass roofed structure provided space for 350 offices and 61 shops. Ramish commissioned the San Francisco firm of MacDonald and Couchot to design the arcade and MacDonald and Kahn as the general contractor. They, in turn, contracted with Gladding, McBean to manufacture Granitex terra cotta for the Spring and Broadway Streets facade. The pottery began work on February 9, 1923, and promised MacDonald and Kahn that the first shipment would be ready by July 15th and the final shipment by September 15th of that year.

Atholl McBean informed the Lincoln staff that this was a rush job and warned them that "Mr. MacDonald is a very difficult man to get along with, and almost impossible to please." Atholl's words turned out to be prophetic. To speed things along, the San Francisco office of the pottery took the unusual step of subcontracting with San Francisco Plastering and Lathing Company to do the modeling for the main facade of the arcade. The pottery supplied the subcontractor with the necessary clay, modeling boards and plans. P. O. Tognelli, however, supervised the work.

For one reason or the other, the pottery did not make its contracted deadline. A delay of approximately two months raised the ire of MacDonald and Kahn, as it allegedly cost them $1,000 for each day lost. On September 20 and 21, Alan MacDonald wrote Atholl two scathing letters denouncing his company for the delay saying "You have damaged us about $100,000.00. . . . Our welfare, however, is in your hands. It is too late now to buy the terra cotta from someone else." MacDonald further stated in the second letter that Gladding, McBean was selected without competition because of being the best in the state but that "apparently contracted time of delivery meant nothing." What the outcome of this torrent of invective was is not known, but it does illustrate the sometimes prickly relationship between the manufacturer and a general contractor.

Apparently MacDonald's harsh words had little effect on the crew back in Lincoln. An interoffice memo from Los Angeles dated just five days later reported that "the terra cotta is going up very fast" and the setting on the tenth floor was just about complete. The end result again seemed to win accolades for the pottery. The Mercantile Arcade, by early 1924, stood as one of the city's most imaginative and striking business and shopping complexes. A congratulatory memo from an unidentified Tropico supervisor to Lincoln admirably expressed the success of the job:

You have perhaps already been complimented on the excellence of the work on the Mercantile Arcade. Yesterday I spent quite a little time looking at it again and I am sure that another word of commendation is not out of place. The job is certainly a peach, and the arches over the entrance are especially effective, and fit perfectly. . . . Personally, I think the gray Granitex color is a little too cold for this town, and I am anxious to see how the Hill Street Building in the Pink Granitex will compare with the Mercantile Arcade.

While the production of architectural terra cotta for these huge downtown office buildings consumed much of the corporation's energy, the pottery also developed a product line for smaller establishments. In 1927, the Tropico Plant published a catalog for stock architectural terra cotta "developed for the purpose of facilitating the use of Terra Cotta on the smaller buildings where lowest costs and shortest deliveries consistent with good manufacturing are imperative." Both the Glendale and Lincoln plants carried stock molds for urns, ornaments, cartouches, pilasters, ashlar, cresting, panels, cornices, and architraves. Available in a cream enamel finish, the stock items could be delivered within a week to ten days of an order. For an additional 25%, the company would produce pieces in polychrome. Examples of stock terra cotta produced by these two plants appeared on the facades of automobile dealerships, schools, banks, hotels, and businesses throughout the West.

By the close of the 1920s, architectural styles evolved from the Beaux Arts to the Parisian Zigzag Moderne. According to David Gebhard in his *The Richfield Building 1928–1968,* Los Angeles boasted three monuments to this futuristic form: the Los Angeles City Hall, Bullock's Wilshire department store, and the Richfield Oil Building. The Los Angeles and Lincoln kilns of Gladding, McBean and Company manufactured the terra cotta for all three. This trio of buildings represented the company's range of capabilities. They incorporated sophisticated modeling for heroic statues, quantities of varicolored ashlar or blocks for the facades, and the best of decorative tile. Based on the job order book in Lincoln, materials for the City Hall and Richfield Building were produced in Los Angeles or Glendale and the terra cotta for Bullock's in Lincoln.

Architects John C. Austin, Albert C. Martin, and John Parkinson received the commission for the City Hall building in 1925. As with other giant buildings of the time, the firm melded a variety of building materials. For the base, from the sidewalk to the top of the second floor, the building was faced with granite of "remarkably fine quality." However, to sheath the 450-foot high structure entirely of granite far exceeded the budget, and consequently the architects turned to terra cotta to harmonize with the gray stone. For its great tower and two flanking wings, the Tropico Plant furnished 3000 tons of enameled finished terra cotta colored a light cream flecked with black. The flanking wings were crowned with the pottery's Cordova roofing tile in a finish of fire-flashed reds, browns and old golds.

What also made this monument particularly pleasing for Gladding, McBean was its heavy use of Tropico decorative tile. A competitor, the Malibu Potteries, also contracted to provide decorative tile for twenty-three large panels and lunettes. Artisans installed rich blue-green decorative tiles for the arcade of the forecourt. Smaller arcade panels of tile were used to illustrate the major activities of the city. For the soffit or undersurface of the arcade, Tropico created a special tile of light blue with gray accents and a tooled surface. Its floor was composed of Promenade tile and the court itself paved in brick. The company magazine *Shapes of Clay,* proudly stated: "All of the products named are from the kilns of Gladding, McBean and Company."

The great rotunda remains as eloquent testimony to the beauty and effectiveness of decorative tile. Edward F. O'Day, the pottery's editor and chief publicist described the rotunda as follows:

The rotunda is the chief interior feature of the building, and the architects enriched it with special opulence. For the dome they chose a tile treatment archaic Greek in design, and Greek in color — ivory, golden buff, pink-tan, and deep crimson terra cotta. The effect is of surprising loveliness, and the student is delighted to preserve the adaptability of old world beauty to a building that will forever dominate the newest of New World cities. It may be said in passing that this dome of decorative tile is the most important achievement in that medium thus far credited to Gladding, McBean and Company.

Completion of the City Hall in 1928 represented a singular achievement for Gladding, McBean. Terra cotta stood out as the most prominant material in a building that dominated the Los Angeles skyline for decades. Naturally, company advertisements in trade magazines featured the new city hall and boasted of the "matchless beauty of terra-cotta."

Simply called Job Order Number 2225 by Lincoln, the Bullock's Wilshire department store was one of their most notable 1920s projects and was hailed as an "unmistakable advance in the movement of contemporary architecture," John and Donald B. Parkinson conceived the design for this ultimate Art Deco store. P. J. Walker was the builder.

For this "contemporary cathedral of commerce," the Lincoln plant manufactured over a thousand tons of standard and polychrome terra cotta. The steel-framed structure with its tall, narrow 241 foot tower featured not only terra cotta but also green metal (copper), black marble, and glass. Gladding, McBean's full-page advertisement in *California Arts and Architecture* provided the best description of their contribution: "Like the rest of this structure moderne, the entrance is clothed in our terra-cotta, unusually large

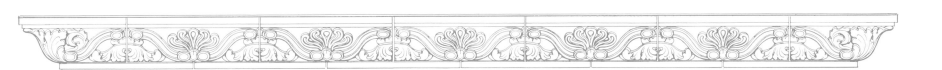

ashlar [rectangular blocks], very rough-hewn, with vertically tooled weathered surface, deep buff in color." The tops of the piers were terra cotta chevrons, and over the main entrance was a stylized sculpted terra cotta panel of eight figures.

"The spirit leaps with the upspringing loveliness of this great building—a terra-cotta masterpiece." These ebullient words reflect the pride of Gladding, McBean's contribution to the Richfield Oil Building. Long a city landmark, completion of this black and gold tower in 1929 culminated the pottery's finest achievement during the Art Deco era.

The Southern Division of the company undertook the project. Designed by Morgan, Walls and Clements and built by P. J. Walker Company, this twelve story structure at 555 South Flower Street incorporated set backs and a massive tower resembling an oil derrick emblazoned on all sides with the word "Richfield." Because of its location away from other tall buildings (at least when it was constructed), the building was finished in terra cotta on all four sides.

The selection of colors by the architects, however, gave the building a unique sense of drama. They chose a combination that suggested the black of oil and the company's colors of blue and gold. This unprecedented combination on such large surfaces presented the pottery with a severe test. According to *Shapes of Clay,* company color experts, ceramic artists, and kiln masters all worked on the problem. Having produced acceptable samples, this team of craftsmen went on to manufacture 800 tons of terra cotta burned in black, gold and blue. For the piers, the company "manufactured a special black enamel ashlar, surfaced with vertical flutes to enliven the play of light and shadow." The architects complemented the black terra cotta with recessed spandrels of polished glass against sheet metal.

To further dazzle the eye, Morgan, Walls and Clements introduced long vertical terra cotta shafts coated in metallic gold between each paired group of windows. The play of the gold ornamentation against satiny black made this building, according to Gebhard, "the perfect example of the 'vertical skyscraper' style." To produce the golden surface, the pottery came up with a new non-tarnishable glaze. As explained by Harris Allen in his "Terra Cotta Versus Terra Firma" (*California Arts & Architecture,* February 1930):

For the gold coat, the terra cotta received a layer of finely pulverized gold particles held in suspension in a transparent glazing solution. This compound is fused on the surface of the individual blocks and forms a permanent coating of great brilliance.

If this were not enough, the pottery produced a rich blue terra cotta to neighbor the gold and tone its lustre. The architects topped the building with chevrons of blue and black and golden parapets of voluted forms.

A building of this magnitude demanded additional decoration. The powerful oil company commissioned Haig Patigian of San Francisco and Metropolitan Life Insurance Company fame to create a series of statues for the main entrance and parapets. Over the main east entrance, the sculptor modeled four figures symbolizing Aviation, Postal Service, Industry and Navigation. These highly stylized figures of gold terra cotta formed the focal point of an elaborate gold terra cotta architrave. Equally dramatic was the procession of heroic nine-foot high human figures symbolizing Motive Power. Gazing downward from the parapets, each stood on a pedestal that rose from secondary columns held at the base by golden caryatids. Presumably, Tognelli and staff created the full-size models for these striking figures of clay. Their shipment and installation combined with Patigian's sometime difficult personality must have caused more than one moment of nervousness for the terra cotta works.

Perhaps inspired by scripture, Gladding, McBean's advertising writers claimed: "Out of our kilns emerged this beauty that 'endureth forever' in everlasting terra cotta." Ironically, the wrecking ball of progress brought down this beauty of "everlasting" black and gold in 1968 and 1969.

Gladding, McBean, through its Lincoln and Los Angeles plants, generated quantities of glistening polychrome and matte-glazed terra cotta in zigzag, floral and geometric patterns for several other of the city's most majestic Art Deco era buildings. Important examples include the Fox-Chicago Realty Building of S. Tilden Norton; the jade green Sun Realty Store & Office Building designed by Claud Beelman; yellow and gold polychrome for the J. J. Newberry store in Hollywood; light buff mottled terra cotta for the imposing fourth home of the Title Guarantee Building of John and Donald Parkinson; and blue green ceramic veneer sheathing for the striking Pellissier Building which contained the Wiltern Theater.

Next to the Richfield Building, the most dramatic addition to the downtown skyline was the 264-foot Eastern and Columbia Outfitting Company's skyscraper at 9th and Broadway. Beginning in December 1929, the Tropico Plant manufactured 978 tons of terra cotta for the project. A bold and brilliant ziggurat of dazzling blue, green and gold ceramic veneer, the Claud Beelman-designed department store featured long fluted piers, geometric and stylized details and a glorious terra cotta entrance. Like the Richfield project, the use of gold terra cotta accents for the entrance, spandrels, grill work and clock tower articulated a majesty symbolic of the city's largest department store.

Educational institutions were frequently clients of Gladding, McBean. In northern California, the pottery manufactured terra cotta for Stanford, University of California, St. Mary's College and College of the Pacific as well as for scores of secondary schools. Southern California proved equally receptive. When the University of California opened its Westwood campus near Los Angeles in 1929, two architectural firms, George W. Kelham, and Allison and Allison designed buildings showing a pronounced Italian Romanesque influence. This style, of course, was tailor-made for the pottery, and the products of its many kilns were incorporated into the designs for Royce Hall, the Library, Physics and Biology Building, Education Building, and Women's and Men's Gymnasium buildings. The heart of the new campus consisted of buildings clad in creamy gray terra cotta, salmon toned face brick and Cordova and Granada roof tile. Decorative tile from the Tropico works decorated the entrance foyer of the Library. For the nearby campus of the University of Southern California, company terra cotta, roofing tile and face brick embellished Mudd Hall and the Student Union Building.

As the company entered the 1930s in the southland, it faced an economy slowed by the Depression and an architectural community with evolving tastes. Projects like the Richfield Building and U.C.L.A. were well underway before the great crash, but even with this downturn the company sustained itself. In this decade, however, the work demanded of its draftsmen and modelers underwent drastic changes. Now architects came back to Gladding, McBean to reface once ornate buildings in relatively plain or simple ceramic veneer or for decorative tile and especially for its world-famous roofing tile. One of the most dramatic examples was the modernizing of the Pacific Mutual Building at Sixth and Olive Streets. Built in 1908 as a classic Beaux Arts structure festooned with ornate capitals, panels, cartouches and cornice, the building's original architect John Parkinson and his son Donald, stripped the facade of its terra cotta frills in 1937 and replaced them with grayish buff ceramic veneer. Proud of their adaptability to new styles, Gladding, McBean praised the architects:

Practical modernity is the keynote of the remodeled Pacific Mutual Building on Los Angeles' busiest street corner. The simple severity of its new lines, the modern feeling of its fluted piers, and the ground-floor shops that yield important rentals to the building's owners are a three-fold tribute to the creative genius of its architects.

Company job orders no longer recorded tons of terra cotta but square feet of tile, and advertisements in architectural and design magazines emphasized pottery, roofing and floor tile, and multi-colored machine-made ceramic veneer. A 1932 advertisement clearly stated the reality of a new era: "Modernizing old buildings means new work for architects; greater values for real estate. Refacing with terra cotta or tile means a modern and up-to-date exterior. Let us help you with suggestions."

Over the following decades, the company reaped profits from a variety of architectural products but nothing like during the era prior to 1930. In 1956, however, it contracted to produce ceramic veneer for a most unusual project, the Fort Moore Memorial. By this time, the modeling crew at Lincoln had been reduced to one man, Ernest Kadel, and the task before him equalled in magnitude the highly reticulated Beaux Arts theaters and business blocks of the 1920s.

The city of Los Angeles commissioned this memorial to honor the raising of the American Flag over Los Angeles on July 4, 1847, and the heroics of the famed Mormon Battalion. A jury selected Kazumi Adachi and Dike Nagano of Los Angeles as architects and awarded well-known Connecticut sculptor Henry Kreis the commission to produce a suitable bas-relief. Adachi and Nagano's imaginative design called for a 400 foot-long, 45 foot-high wall with a waterfall and 68 foot-high pylon surmounted with a giant American eagle. The far left-hand side of the wall would carry the Kreis sculpture.

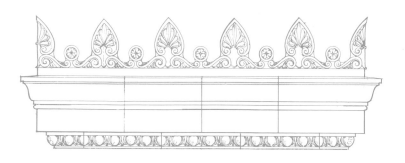

Early in 1956, Gladding, McBean and Company began work on the massive wall. A letter dated January 30 from M. A. Daly of the Los Angeles division indicated that the pottery would be required to produce approximately seventy tons of hand made ceramic veneer and 1,460 square feet of "Anchor type" ceramic veneer at a total cost of $68,500. Daly also wrote that Lincoln would do the drafting and colors would be selected later.

While the production of the terra cotta blocks represented a large order, the real test lay with the creation of Kreis' bas-relief. The sculptor's highly stylized design depicted American troops raising the flag and a series of flanking vignettes showing other elements important in the region's history, including orange groves, cattle ranches, methods of transportation, spiritual life, and modern water and power systems. Kreis was fortunate to have a man of Kadel's expert knowledge and experience in Lincoln. Kadel had worked in the modeling department during the glory days of architectural terra cotta and had the benefit of learning from DeGolyer and Tognelli.

According to an article in *Architectural Ceramics* (September 1958), it took Kadel and his Lincoln assistants two years to translate the Connecticut sculptor's models into their final glazed terra cotta form.

Thirty tons of modeling clay were used in making the original clay model. Upon completion, the model was cut into segments of exacting measurements and a plaster mold made of each segment. Clay was then forced into the molds to form the sections. After the drying, the pieces were glazed, fired and given a final fitting.

Its size must have overwhelmed the modeling rooms and strained the great easel. A photograph of several of the panels fitted together shows Kadel being dwarfed by the pioneers of 1847. In one letter, he complained that he had to lay off one person due to lack of space. By the time Kadel and his crew had finished, 639 glazed pieces were assembled in the fitting house for final inspection. Along the way, of course, staff made routine adjustments such as changing the lettering from "First Dragoons" to "1st Dragoons". Photographs sent to Kreis and others involved with the project invariably elicited criticism for "grotesque legs" and shoe soles of the wrong thickness.

Finally, Kadel sent the carefully packed pieces to the building site for installation. Once completed, the 45 by 75 foot mural received acclaim as the largest bas-relief panel in the country. Using essentially the same techniques established generations before, this job, under Kadel's skillful direction, ranks as one of the architectural terra cotta department's proudest and most visible achievements.

Throughout the first half of the twentieth century and especially prior to the Great Depression, the city of Los Angeles and its neighboring communities provided Gladding, McBean with some of its most spectacular examples of architectural terra cotta. The pottery's job order book in Lincoln listed over 400 jobs in the city alone, and its magazine boasted that Los Angeles pulsed to "the rhythm of terra-cotta." In a 1926 issue of *California Southland,* which featured a painting of a Gladding, McBean project on the cover, a headline stated that in "the southland of California . . . its towns are terra cotta towns." As well, the company's Lincoln and Los Angeles area kilns churned out architectural terra cotta for dozens of smaller job orders in Pasadena, Hollywood, Santa Monica, Beverly Hills, Anaheim, and Riverside and Ventura.

Shields for Spreckels Building, San Diego, 1925

SAN DIEGO

While it did not manufacture terra cotta for San Diego on a scale comparable with that for Los Angeles, Gladding, McBean did significant work in the picturesque oceanside city. Examples are the Cabrillo Theater, Scripps Building, San Diego Gas and Electric Building, San Diego Trust and Savings Bank, and the Helix Building. Before its takeover by Gladding, McBean in 1924, the Los Angeles Pressed Brick Company also produced terra cotta for several San Diego structures, including the highly ornamented facade of the Pantages Theater.

One job that Gladding, McBean took great pride in was the Spreckels Building on Broadway between 6th and 7th streets. In fact, editor Edward F. O'Day devoted an entire issue of *Shapes of Clay* to the Beaux Arts skyscraper. The Spreckels family, of course, was most familiar with the work of the pottery as demonstrated by their San Francisco office buildings and mansions. The giant transpacific company commissioned John D. and Donald B. Parkinson of Los Angeles as architects and Edwards, Wildey and Dixon as general contractors for the 13 story office building, which was to be named for John D. Spreckels of the San Diego branch of the family.

In many respects, the Spreckels Building was a typical 1920s office building similar to many terra cotta clad skyscrapers in San Francisco, Los Angeles, Fresno, Oakland and Sacramento. What made this a challenge, however, was the fact that this port city did not have many tall buildings. Consequently, the building's tremendous height and mass and relationship to its neighbors required that it be viewed from all sides. Two banks representing Spreckels financial interests would occupy the ground floor, and the architects planned the top story or penthouse to house a businessmen's club. In general concept, the Los Angeles firm modeled the Spreckels Building after the early Renaissance palaces of Tuscany. "The architects felt," wrote O'Day, "that the style might properly be adapted to a modern office building, on account of the case with which the endless repetition of typical office windows could be effected in such a simple rusticated wall, relieved only by refined and unobtrusive detail."

Architectural terra cotta lent itself handsomely to the design of this Renaissance style building. Gladding, McBean's contract called for the production of terra cotta for its massive astylar (columnless) facades, belt courses, ornamental balconies, and a richly detailed projecting cornice. Three of the elevations would be clothed in gray Granitex ashlar and the fourth in a combination of terra cotta and gray face brick. Included in the specifications were such decorative features as a heraldic name shield above the main entrance way, two large heraldic shields depicting a Spanish galleon and modern vessel at the corners between the ninth and tenth floors and two gargoyles attached to corners of the cornice. The San Francisco office promised the first shipment on January 15, 1926 and the final one on May 1.

Work on the Spreckels Building, while somewhat routine, also included several features that well illustrate many of the complex steps and occasional problems encountered in creating sophisticated ornamentation. By January 26, 1925, the drafting room in Lincoln received Parkinson and Parkinson's detailed drawings and work began in earnest. The Tropico office in Los Angeles served as the liaison between the architect and Lincoln. A memo from Herbert Brown at Tropico to the modeling department shows how the company's library of architectural plate books played a useful role. In this dispatch, Brown states that the architects suggested that Kadel look at the plates in *Details for the Architecture of Tuscany* for the balcony brackets and *Byzantine Art in Italy* for the ornament belt. For the more difficult panels between the cornice brackets and the heraldic shields, however, the architects supplied their own detailed drawings. Even with these drawings, however, architects made mistakes as noted in the following memorandum:

We hand you herewith sketches received from Mr. Parkinson for the cornice panels and the shields. Mr. Parkinson advises us that after the drawings were made they discovered that the Galley on the 10th story shield had an English poop instead of a square one such as exists in the Spanish examples. Please have your modeler make this correction when he executes the work.

Mr. Parkinson would like to see all of these models in a very incomplete state to be sure that the modeler is getting the spirit he wishes in the work.

As demonstrated by the Spreckels Building, a terra cotta works faced numerous logistical obstacles. Once the finished terra cotta left Lincoln, the company's responsibility was by no means concluded. Frequently, building sites did not have sufficient space to store the finished terra cotta before it was set. In the case of the Spreckels Building, the pottery had to make arrangements with the R. E. Hazard Company of San Diego to store and haul the terra cotta from the railroad to the building site. Further, constant memos were sent from the building site to Lincoln requesting replacements and patching for pieces that arrived broken or chipped. Seemingly, in every job, a small percentage of the terra cotta arrived damaged, but since Lincoln kept the molds, this did not represent a serious problem. The Spreckels job also identified another quality-control problem faced by a pottery: staining. Workers in Lincoln wrapped the terra cotta in cardboard and straw for shipment on railroad cars. One message expressed worry that rain would cause the cardboard to stain the pieces in Hazard's yards while another reported that wet packing straw had stained the gray Granitex yellow.

Early in 1927, in spite of these minor setbacks, Gladding, McBean finished work on the huge office building and noted with considerable satisfaction the beauty and significance of their product. The pottery advertised the building in the architectural and design magazines and, as mentioned before, featured it in the December 1927 issue of *Shapes of Clay*. One of the primary reasons, of course, was that the company hoped to generate additional business in the region. No doubt, this Renaissance business palace directly influenced the selection of Gladding, McBean for San Diego's next major skyscraper, the San Diego Trust and Savings Bank. O'Day, in the opening paragraph of his magazine, summarized the importance of the Spreckels Building not only to San Diego but also implicitly to the pottery:

Architecturally and commercially the John D. Spreckels Building of San Diego is one of the outstanding structures of southern California. In beautiful San Diego it stands alone at present, but surely may be regarded as the first item in a program of commercial building that is destined to express, within a short time, the rapidly growing importance of this great Western American seaport.

BEYOND CALIFORNIA

While most of Gladding, McBean's projects were in California, the company produced architectural terra cotta for buildings in cities across the Pacific Slope. Beginning in the 1880s and stretching into the late 1920s, the booming Pacific Northwest cities of Vancouver, Victoria, Seattle, Portland, Spokane and Tacoma developed into a particularly successful region for the architectural department. Portland, for example, was the site of 110 Lincoln projects and Seattle 95. Only San Francisco and Los Angeles exceeded this number. Architects from both California cities who had worked with Gladding, McBean designed buildings for the Pacific Northwest and this undoubtedly helped the pottery win jobs in the region.

Portland featured, among other Gladding, McBean jobs, the Yeon Building, U.S. National Bank, Journal Building, Wells Fargo Building, and Multnomah County Courthouse. Important projects in Seattle included the 42-story L. C. Smith tower, Pioneer Building, Dexter Horton Building, Olympic Hotel, Hoge Building, and the Federal Office Building. So important to Gladding, McBean was its northwest business that the company strengthened its hold by acquiring the Northern Clay Company plant in Auburn, Washington, in 1925 and merging with Denny-Renton Clay & Coal Company of Washington in 1927.

The pottery produced tons of architectural terra cotta for the illustrious Hotel Utah, Deseret National Bank, and University of Utah in Salt Lake City as well as for dozens of buildings from Ogden to Provo. In Kansas City, the elegant Orpheum Theater of George Lansburg represented one of Gladding, McBean's greatest achievements. Arizona was represented by the Maricopa County Courthouse and City Hall, U.S. Post Office, and National Bank of Arizona in Phoenix. Several buildings for the University of Arizona, including the Stewart Observatory in Tucson, incorporated burnt clay from Lincoln.

In Hawaii, the Waikiki Beach Hotel and Alexander & Baldwin Ltd. Building were both Gladding, McBean projects. Further across the Pacific, the Japanese incorporated Lincoln terra cotta on the Tokyo buildings of the Japan Oil Company, Nippon Yusen Kaisha and Mitsubishi Banking

Hall. In 1916, The Union Steamship Company Building of Sydney, Australia clad its stately headquarters with 462 tons of terra cotta. No doubt shipping problems, replacement of chipped pieces, and supervision from afar mitigated against active pursuit of overseas jobs.

When the stock market crashed in 1929 and the economy slipped into the Great Depression of the 1930s, many well-known terra cotta companies went out of business. Gladding, McBean and Company survived, but just barely. Company stock which sold for 98½ per share in 1929 bottomed out at 3⅞ in 1932, and net earnings plummeted from over $1.1 million to $149,000 in one year. Through salary reductions, omission of dividends, and conversion of assets into cash, the company fought for survival until the mid-1930s when the national economy showed new signs of life. In 1934, the corporation reorganized, moved its corporate headquarters to Los Angeles (although the Lincoln plant remained active) and Atholl McBean was named chairman of the board rather than president.

Two clay products that helped Gladding, McBean through those difficult years were ceramic veneer and face brick. Ceramic veneer, economical to make, clothed such well-known structures as the Federal Building and United States Post Office in the Los Angeles Civic Center, City College of San Francisco, the Federal Building in San Francisco's civic center, University of California Medical Center, the Veteran's Administration Hospital in Seattle, and Condon Hall of the University of Washington. Gladding, McBean face brick was used on the Beverly Hills Post Office, McLaren Lodge in Golden Gate Park and the UCLA School of Law Building.

In its 1937 issue of *Shapes of Clay* (the magazine was revived after an absence of five years during the Depression), the company pointed out that in addition to the above architectural materials, its famous Hermosa tile and the development of Franciscan earthenware pulled them through and ensured future prosperity. Through the 1933 purchase of the American Encaustic Tiling Company plants in Hermosa Beach and Vernon and acquisition of patent rights, the company developed new shapes, sizes, and colors of Hermosa Real Clay Tile. In addition, to meet heavy demands, the Glendale plant expanded to become the company's largest factory. Architects and contractors employed tile in thousands of homes and businesses. Prominent examples include white Hermosa Tile for the

San Francisco-Oakland Bay Bridge tunnel, the exterior facing of the National Broadcasting Building in San Francisco, Bullock's Department Store in Westwood and the lobby of Alexander and Baldwin Ltd. in Honolulu.

During the next decades, the pottery continued to acquire other companies, add new equipment, and market its large and varied product line. Gladding, McBean opened sales rooms in every major Western city and in Chicago and New York. In the production of tile and sewer pipe it remained the largest manufacturer west of the Mississippi. But with bigness came other fundamental changes. Atholl McBean stepped down as chairman in 1953. Earlier the Gladding family's formal association with the firm had ended when the sons of Albert founded the Gladding Brothers Manufacturing Company in San Jose in 1929.

Even while the corporation had expanded far and wide, the original works back in Lincoln also had expanded, and by 1930 more than 20 acres of floor space were under roof. Throughout the years, the Lincoln staff continued to manufacture its standard products: sewer pipe, roofing tile, ceramic veneer, earthenware, chimney pipe, garden pottery and newer products like Franciscan Terra Floor. Levels of production ebbed and flowed with the popularity of each commodity. Occasionally, the architectural staff under Ernest Kadel took on projects recalling the glory days of architectural terra cotta such as the Fort Moore Monument in Los Angeles and figures for the Los Angeles County Court House. The Lincoln payroll reached a peak of 750 in 1948, but technological developments gradually reduced the required number of employees to less than 250.

Over the generations, Gladding, McBean had acquired a succession of plants up and down the Pacific Coast. In 1962, the tables turned when it merged with Lock Joint Pipe Company to form Interpace Corporation. Then, in 1976, Interpace sent shockwaves through Lincoln when it announced the closure of the plant—101 years after its founding. Fortunately this dire situation did not last long. Pacific Coast Building Products of Sacramento stepped in, purchased the Lincoln plant, and restored the operation to its former vitality. "Today," so states a company brochure, "the plant is thriving, manufacturing vitrified clay pipe, roof tile, architectural terra cotta, split pavers and tile veneers. With proven clay reserves assuring operations for decades to come . . . Gladding, McBean & Co. is alive and well!"

Sculptor Tom Collins with Eagle for The Great Lakes Naval Base, Chicago, 1988

MAKING TERRA COTTA

The Process From Clay Pit to Cornice

The following is a composite of period articles that appeared in trade journals between 1876 and 1915. Their purpose was to acquaint architects and builders with the process of manufacturing terra cotta when its architectural and decorative applications were relatively new. Although changes in technology have altered the process somewhat, esentially it is still the labor-intensive craft described here.

Architectural terra cotta begins as lowly clay, the sediment of millennia deposited on ancient lake and river beds. It is mined by the laborious methods used to extract coal or raw ore and transported to the terra cotta manufactory in loose powder form. Once it enters the storage bins, it begins the long process of becoming finished terra cotta. The clay is first washed in a *blunging-tub,* a large circular metal tub containing a belt-driven mixer. Here the clay is mixed with water to the consistency of cream, a known quantity of clay being used for each mixing. The slip thus formed passes through a strainer in the side of the tub, into a brick receiving vat below. The stone and other impurities in the clay remain at the bottom of the tub. As soon as the contents of one blunging tub have been run off into the vat, other constituents of the terra cotta, proportioned to the amount of clay, are spread over the deposit. Then another washing takes place; the constituents are spread in the vat, and the process continues until the vat is full, the superfluous water rising to the top. The water is then drawn off, leaving a paste which is allowed to stand as long as possible, sometimes up to a full year. The paste when required for use is cut through vertically, and is mixed in *pug-mills* . . . it is then ready for use and is passed over to the molders. While the clay is being prepared the terra cotta manufacturer is busily engaged in other stages of the process.

DRAWING

The project architect supplies the terra cotta manufacturer with a full set of plans. The manufacturer then completely redraws the architect's plans to "terra cotta construction." It is impossible for the architect to do this himself beyond a certain extent, for it requires years of practical experience in the manufacture of terra cotta, knowledge of manufacturing methods of the factory in which the material is to be made, and intimate knowledge of the characteristics of that factory's product, as well as thorough experience in construction and drafting. For instance, all factories do not use the same shrinkage scale,

and in some factories more than one shrinkage scale is used because different colors may require different temperatures, involving a different shrinkage. There are countless other points which must be considered. The shape of the piece, the relation between the dimensions, and the end upon which it is to be set in the kiln, must be thought out carefully so that the piece will burn straight and shrink evenly.

The method of anchoring to the form of frame construction the architect elects must be worked out in detail by factory engineers and draftsmen, and here again intimate knowledge of terra cotta is necessary. The drawings show the size of every anchor, its attachment to the piece with the necessary aperture, and the attachment to the frame. Complete iron schedules are compiled for the iron contractors bid. The dimensions of the bond are given and its connection with the masonry or iron work. All joints are clearly shown, and they differ from stone joints in that possible uneven shrinkage must be taken into account with regard to correcting it after burning. The better class of manufacturers always figure entrance and lower story work, where the joints will be prominent, larger than the actual size necessary to permit grinding the joints by machinery to mechanical exactness.

The scale drawings are sent to the architect for approval, and on return full size drawings are made to shrinkage call for the use of the modelers and molders.

MODELS AND MOLDS

When the terra cotta calls for ornament or figure design, the model is made in clay by hand. Sometimes the architect indicates roughly the style of ornament desired, and leaves it to the manufacturer to develop the design in detail. For this reason the manufacturer must maintain the highest quality of skilled labor in the modeling department; frequently the head of the department is a true sculptor who must be conversant with every style of architectural ornament as well. A fully equipped photographic department, which the manufacturer must also maintain, prepares photographs of the models, which the architect approves or revises unless he prefers to inspect the work personally. Even in a completed state the models are subject to his revision. When approval has been received plaster molds are made directly from the models, one for each piece of

(continued on page 136)

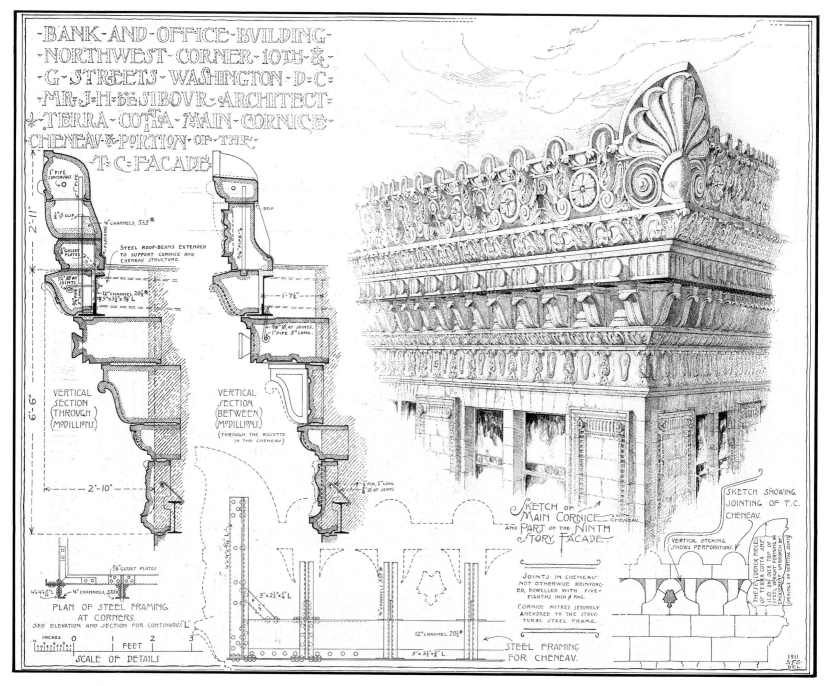

The drawing is titled:

BANK AND OFFICE BUILDING
NORTHWEST CORNER 10TH &
G STREETS WASHINGTON D.C.
MR. J.H. DE SIBOUR ARCHITECT
TERRA COTTA MAIN CORNICE
CHENEAU & PORTION OF THE
T.C. FACADE

Above: A detail drawing from 1911 showing method of attaching terra cotta to structural steel frame of building.

Right: In 1915, the Brickbuilder, *a journal featuring terra cotta applications, sponsored a design contest for a hypothetical hotel to be clad entirely in terra cotta. Many well-known architects entered the competition under colorful aliases. This imaginative submission by "The Black Cat" came from Boston architects George Blount and John Gray.*

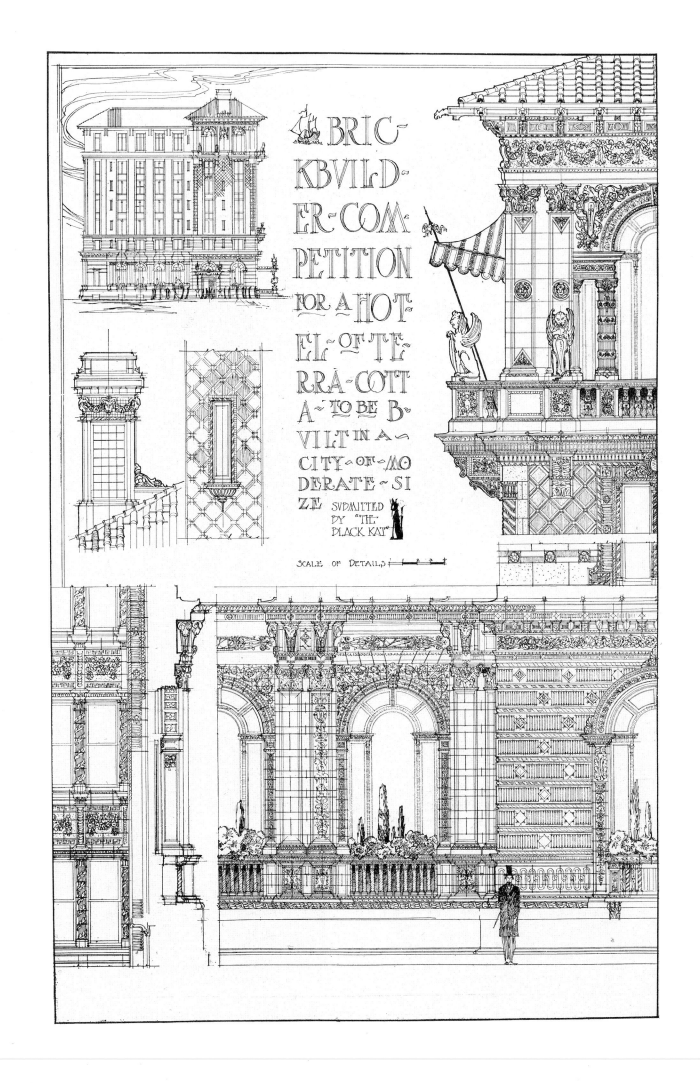

BRIC
KBVILD~
ER~COM~
PETITION
FOR A HOT
EL~OF~TE~
RRA~COTT
A~TO BE B~
VILT IN A~
CITY~OF~MO
DERATE~SI
ZE SVBMITTED
BY "THE
BLACK KAT"

SCALE OF DETAILS

different design; and to expedite the work, or when an unusually large number of exactly similar pieces are required, two or more molds are made. It will be readily seen that great economy in modeling results when a design is so arranged that the ornament frequently repeats.

PRESSING

When the plaster molds are completed and ready for use, prepared terra cotta clay from the pug-mills is pressed into the molds by hand. The pressing does not require especially skilled labor, but must be done under careful supervision to insure that the clay is pressed to the proper thickness. At this stage clay braces, struts, and apertures that will receive the iron anchors are built into each piece. After the moist clay has become firm, usually after a day or so, it is carefully pulled from the plaster mold. Every piece must then be finished by hand with modeling tools. In the case of intricate ornament, it frequently takes as long to finish the piece as it does to press it, and the finisher must possess some knowledge of the essentials of modeling.

DRYING

Before the piece can be colored and burned, it must be thoroughly dried. This is necessarily a slow process at first. Fully one half of the entire shrinkage takes place during drying, and unless this goes on gradually warping is inevitable, and warping started in the drying almost invariably becomes more marked in burning. There is also danger of cracking if heat is applied to soon. However, it is possible to heat the buildings at night above the normal temperature, and drying is further expedited by placing the material in artificially heated tunnels when the process is far enough advanced. The time required to dry a piece of average size is one week. In case of an unusually large piece with dimensions out of proper ratio the time must be doubled.

SPRAYING

When the building is to be of one color, application of color to the terra cotta is a comparatively simple matter. Pigment of the desired color is mixed with clay slip and the slip in liquid form is sprayed on the piece with an atomizer operated by compressed air. In the very simplest colors from two to three coats of one slip are sufficient. The number of slips required varies from one to four — and even five — in the more complex glazes.

In coloring polychrome material the method of application is the same, in general, except that it is a much more delicate operation and requires considerable skill on the part of the operator.

In the preparation of the various colors, the highest kind of technical ceramic chemistry is required. There are no commercial glazes that are suitable for terra cotta and every factory must maintain its own ceramic chemical laboratory. The men at the head of these have in general obtained university degrees in ceramic chemistry and often have studied in Germany or England as well. At best, however, theoretical knowledge obtained in this way serves only as a basis for experiments which must be adapted to local conditions, which not only are not alike in any two factories, but liable to change "without notice."

BURNING

Once the glaze has been applied and is thoroughly dry, the terra cotta pieces are made ready for burning. The kilns in which terra cotta is burned are made with double walls through which the heat circulates, and the flames do not come in contact with the material. Such contact would be absolutely ruinous. Even a small leak admitting gas into the inner chamber is disastrous. The fuel in general use is soft coal. [Gladding, McBean used wood and later, natural gas.] The size of an average kiln is 18 feet diameter and 15 feet high, inside dimensions, with a double wall from 3 to 5 feet through. On the outside the kilns resemble conventional bee hives in general form, save for a flattened roof, and are constructed of fire brick, bound with strong iron bands. Such a kiln will hold from 35 to 45 tons, burned weight.

The terra cotta cannot be set on its face, for the slip or glaze fluxes [liquifies] in burning and adheres firmly to anything with which it comes in contact. The glazed material requires particular care in this respect. As the material is loaded, tiers are built of blocks and slabs of a fire-clay mixture, for terra cotta when it approaches maturity is too near the fluxing point to bear any great superimposed weight. The fire-clay body, having been burned previously at a greater heat than that to which the terra cotta is subjected, can withstand the weight of the terra cotta. Terra cotta reaches a temperature of about 2300 degrees Fahrenheit in the kilns, and at that heat is white-hot and translucent. It is this process that renders it so absolutely fireproof.

It takes from twelve to fourteen days to "turn over" a kiln — one day to load; four days' slow heating, to evaporate any moisture the drying may not have eliminated; four days full heat; four days' cooling and one day to unload.

FITTING

Before shipment all work is laid out in sections and carefully fitted. The better class of manufacturers, by making the pieces too large originally, are able to discount any small inequities of shrinkage by grinding the joints on a steel rubbing bed, with a mechanically accurate result. This, of course, involves an extra expense, generally borne by the manufacturer. It is slight, however, compared to the improvement in appearance. Grinding is hardly necessary for third story and higher work, where the distance from the ground makes any small irregularities unnoticeable. Generally extra pieces have been made to take the place of any broken in the kiln. If necessary replacements are rushed through and burned in a small kiln to save time.

SHIPPING

While terra cotta is a very strong material and when properly set in a building easily stands any compression it is called upon to bear, it is brittle and a sharp blow will chip it. Consequently, the greatest care is necessary when loading cars or barges. The material is packed in straw and firmly braced to prevent dislodgment. The only practical means of transporting terra cotta to extended points is by railroad car, and by deck boats. The material to be carried in holds of steamers must necessarily be crated first, an operation which consumes much time and is costly.

INSTALLATION

Once the material reaches its ultimate destination, it is unloaded from the rail cars, ships or barges and carried by wagon to the building site. There it is carefully unpacked and stored where it will be protected until needed. If all has gone well, the terra cotta pieces will arrive when progress on the building is at the proper point to receive them. Iron or steel anchors, hangars, and structural supports will have been delivered and installed and the masons will be ready and waiting. Setting heavy terra cotta at ground level and on lower floors obviously presents fewer problems than installation high above street level. Cranes and elevators are used to lift the terra cotta sections to their proper positions where masons carefully set each piece and grout and seal the joints. When their work is done the transition from clay pit to cornice is complete — the combined skills of architect, artisan, chemist and mason are merged into a finished enduring addition to the urban landscape.

Excerpts from:
"The Manufacture of Terra Cotta in Chicago," from *The American Architect and Building News,* December 30, 1876

"A History of Architectural Terra Cotta," by Harry Lee King, *The Architect and Engineer,* February, 1914

"Architectural Terra Cotta — Its Physical and Structural Properties," by Edward H. Putnam, *The Brickbuilder,* 1915

BUILDING INDEX

PRINCIPAL CALIFORNIA ARCHITECTURAL PROJECTS OF
GLADDING, MCBEAN MENTIONED IN TEXT

The following list has been extrapolated primarily from the job order books of the Lincoln and Tropico plants. In some cases the names do not correspond to official or popular names of buildings, thus, for example, the Oakland Tribune Tower is listed as Tribune Tower. Occasionally the order books do not record the architect or tonnage. Projects undertaken by the Tropico Plant are designated with a "T" preceeding the job number. A few buildings were not mentioned in either book and are so indicated. Dates represent terra cotta delivery and not building openings.

BUILDING	LOCATION	DATE	ARCHITECT	TONNAGE	JOB
Affiliated Colleges	San Francisco	1896–97	J. E. Kraft	NA	336
Alvarado School	San Francisco	1925	G. A. Lansburgh	167	808
Bacon Land & Loan Company	Oakland	1903	NA	NA	571
Balboa Bldg.	San Francisco	1909	Bliss & Faville	NA	863
Bank of Italy	Los Angeles	1924	Morgan, Walls & Morgan	[Tropico]	
Barker Bros.	Los Angeles	1925	Curlett & Beelman	963.5	1773
Beverly-Wilshire Apts.	Los Angeles	1926	Walker & Eisen	567	T1642
Biltmore Hotel	Los Angeles	1922	Schultz & Weaver	850	1522
Bradbury, L. L. Residence	Los Angeles	1886	S. & J. C. Newsom	NA	76
Braly Bldg. (Union Trust)	Los Angeles	1902	J. Parkinson	420	550
Breuner, John Co.	Oakland	1931	A. F. Foller	259	2381
Bullock & Jones	San Francisco	1923	Reid Bros.	26	1648
Bullock's Wilshire	Los Angeles	1929	J. & D. Parkinson	1212.5	2225
Cabrillo Theater	San Diego	1914	W. S. Keller	15.5	1137
California State Bank	Sacramento	1889	Curlett & Cuthbertson	NA	29
California State Life Insurance	Sacramento	1923	Geo. C. Sellon	532	1618
Capitol Ext. Library & Courts	Sacramento	1922	Weeks & Day	746	1521
Capitol Ext. Office Bldg.	Sacramento	1922	Weeks & Day	674	1520
Central Savings	Oakland	1925	G. W. Kelham	842	1783
Children's Hospital Addn.	San Francisco	1927	Bakewell & Brown	74	2045
Chronicle Bldg.	San Francisco	1888	Burnham & Root	NA	9
College of the Pacific	Stockton	1924	Davis, Heller, Pearce	316.5	1692
Cowell, Henry Bldg.	San Francisco	1914	H. H. Meyers	72	1110
Dollar, Robert Bldg.	San Francisco	1919	Chas. W. McCall	75	1405
Eastern Out-fitting Co.	Los Angeles	1929	C. Beelman	978	T1644
Elks Bldg.	Fresno	1927	Kamp & Johnson	65.5	2058
Elks Bldg.	Sacramento	1925	Hemmings & Starks	330	1782
Fine Arts Bldg.	Los Angeles	1925	Walker & Eisen	NA	
Financial Center Bldg.	Oakland	1929	Reed & Curlett	245	2189
Fireman's Fund Ins. Co.	San Francisco	1914	L. P. Hobart	210	1117
Flood Bldg.	San Francisco	1902	NA	NA	553
Fort Moore Memorial	Los Angeles	1956	K. Adachi & D. Nagano	70	6720
Fox-Chicago Realty Bldg.	Los Angeles	1930	S. T. Norton	313	T1709
Fuller, W. P. & Co.	Sacramento	1924	R. A. Herold	20.5	1746
Garfield Bldg.	Los Angeles	1928	C. Beelman	580	2215
Gladding, A. L.	Lincoln	1913	A. J. Gladding	1	1066
Gladding, McBean & Co.	San Francisco	1884	NA	NA	NA
Griffith-McKenzie Bldg.	Fresno	1913	Geo. W. Kelham	110	1054
Hamburger Bldg.	Los Angeles	1906	A. F. Rosenheim	NA	725
Hart, H. H. Restaurant	Sacramento	1925	Dean & Dean	16	1772
Hearst Bldg.	San Francisco	1910	Kirby, Petit	800	901
Heinemann Bldg.	San Francisco	1909	MacDonald & Applegarth	30	877
Helix Building	San Diego	1897	Bancroft	NA	343
Hellman Bldg.	Los Angeles	1905	A. F. Rosenheim	21.5	694
Herman Davis & Sons	Sacramento	1924	Hemmings & Sparks	1	1705
Hobart Bldg.	San Francisco	1914	Willis Polk & Co.	650	1108
Hollingsworth Bldg.	Los Angeles	1912	Morgan, Walls & Morgan	NA	1021
Hunter-Dulin	San Francisco	1926	Schultze & Weaver	1588	1894
Huntington Apts.	San Francisco	1923	Weeks & Day	191	1644
Insurance Exchange	San Francisco	1912	Willis Polk & Co.	555	1041
Junior Orpheum	Los Angeles	1921	G. A. Lansburgh	430	1478
Junior Orpheum	San Francisco	1920	G. A. Lansburgh	377	1475
Kerckhoff Bldg.	Los Angeles	1915	Morgan, Walls & Morgan	164	1200
Knickerbocker Bldg.	Los Angeles	1913	Austin & Pennell	99	1052
Kress, S. H. & Co.	Oakland	1925	E. T. J. Hoffman	163	1885
Lankershim's Main St. Bldg.	Los Angeles	NA			
Lincoln Grammar School	Lincoln	1921	Geo. C. Sellon & Co.	2	1482
Loew's State Theater	Los Angeles	1920	G. Lansburgh	427	1470
Loew's State Theater	San Francisco	1920	G. Lansburgh	465	1469
Los Angeles Athletic Club	Los Angeles	1911	Parkinson & Bergstrom	150	927
Los Angeles City Hall	Los Angeles	1925	Austin, Martin & Parkinson	3000	T1116
Los Angeles Trust & Sav. Bank	Los Angeles	1910	Parkinson & Bergstrom	655	894
Mark Hopkins Hotel	San Francisco	1925	Weeks & Day	546	1876
Masonic Temple	San Francisco	1910	Bliss & Faville	240	977
Matson Bldg.	San Francisco	1920	Bliss & Faville	860	1471
McBean Memorial	Lincoln	1925	Dean & Dean	6.5	1781
Memorial Auditorium	Sacramento	1925	Dean, Lansburgh & Brown	100	1865

BUILDING	LOCATION	DATE	ARCHITECT	TONNAGE	JOB
Mercantile Arcade	Los Angeles	1923	MacDonald & Couchot	507	1621
Metropolitan Life Ins. Co.	San Francisco	1919	J. R. Miller	750	1417
Mills Bldg.	San Francisco	1890	Burnham & Root	NA	112
Mission H. S. Additions	San Francisco	1925	J. Reid, Jr.	268	1864
Music Stand Golden Gate Park	San Francisco	1899	NA	NA	422
Native Sons Hall	Sacramento	1916	W. J. Miller	30	1262
Native Sons Hall Main Entrance	Sacramento	1917	W. J. Miller	8.5	1285
Native Sons Hall	San Francisco	1911	Righetti & Headman	15	954
Newberry, J. J. Store	Hollywood	1929	Hoffman	27	T1607
Newhall Bldg.	San Francisco	1905	L. P. Hobart	NA	NA
Oakland City Hall	Oakland	1911	Palmer & Hornbostel	960	955
Oakland Gas & Light & Heat Co.	Oakland	1892	Coxhead & Coxhead	NA	188
O'Conner-Moffat	San Francisco	1928	L. P. Hobart	411	2102
Opera House, War Memorial	San Francisco	1931	Arthur Brown, Jr.; G. A. Lansburgh	NA	2386
Orpheum Theater	Los Angeles	1911	G. A. Lansburgh	123	905
Pacific Gas & Electric Bldg.	San Francisco	1923	Bakewell & Brown	1010	1689
Pacific Mutual	Los Angeles	1925	Schultze & Weaver	530	1861
Pacific Tel. & Tel. Co.	Fresno	1925	R. F. Felchlin Co.	47	1813
Pacific Tel. & Tel. Bldg. Addn.	Sacramento	1924	Bliss & Faville	25	1702
Pacific Tel. & Tel. Bldg.	San Francisco	1924	Miller & Pflueger	3200	1699
Pacific Tel. & Tel Bldg.	Oakland	1895	NA	NA	279
Pacific Southwest Trust & Sav. Bank	Fresno	1923	R. F. Felchlin Co.	492	1668
Pantages Theater	Los Angeles	1919	B. Marcus Priteca	560	1410
Paramount Theater	Oakland	1931	Pflueger	67	WU# 1
Pellissier Bldg.	Los Angeles	1930	Morgan, Walls & Morgan	132	T1727
Pioneer Hall	San Francisco	1885	Wright & Sanders	NA	NA
Post Inquirer Bldg.	Oakland	1927	J. Morgan	31.5	2078
Radin & Kamp Dept. Store	Fresno	1924	R. F. Felchlin	92.5	1750
Raphael Weill School	San Francisco	1926	Meyer & Johnson	NA	1961
Richfield Oil Bldg.	Los Angeles	1928	Morgan, Walls & Clements	800	T1463
Roos Bros.	Oakland	1922	Wm. Knowles	163	1597
Roosevelt Bldg.	Los Angeles	1926	Curlett & Beelman	840	T949
Rowell Bldg.	Fresno	1912	E. T. Foulkes	46	1031
Russ Bldg.	San Francisco	1926	G. W. Kelham	3740	1919
Sacramento Pub. Library Bldg.	Sacramento	1917	L. P. Rixford	167	1295
St. Brigid's Church Alts.	San Francisco	1930	H. A. Minton	23.5	2340
St. Dominic's Church	San Francisco	c.1927	Beezer Bros.	NA	NA
St. Mary's Cemetery Gateway	Oakland	1893	NA	NA	242
St. Mary's College Bldg.	Oakland	1889	J. J. Clark	NA	27
San Diego Gas & Electric Bldg.	San Diego	1897	Zimmer & Reamer	NA	366
San Diego Trust Sav. Bank	San Diego	1927	W. F. Johnson	557	2021
San Francisco City Hall	San Francisco	1913	Bakewell & Lawson	230	1105
San Francisco Public Library	San Francisco	1915	G. W. Kelham	21	1195
San Joaquin Light & Power	Fresno	1922	R. F. Felchlin	416	1616
Senator Hotel	Sacramento	1923	MacDonald & Couchot	88.5	1676
Scripps Bldg.	San Diego	1907	NA	NA	769
Southern Pacific Bldg.	San Francisco	1916	Bliss & Faville	769	1256
Southern Pacific Station	Oakland	1911	Jarvis Hunt	350	957
Spreckels, Claus Bldg.	San Francisco	1897	Reid Bros.	NA	339
Spreckels, J. D. Residence	San Francisco	1898	Reid Bros.	NA	NA
Spreckels, J. D. Bldg.	San Diego	1924	J. & D. Parkinson	1300	1767
Standard Oil Bldg.	San Francisco	1920	G. W. Kelham	2200	1473
Stanford Univ.	Palo Alto	1899 – 1935	[24 separate job orders]		
Story Bldg.	Los Angeles	1908	Morgan & Walls	NA	819
Sun Realty Store & Office	Los Angeles	1930	C. Beelman	210	T1672
Title Guarantee Bldg.	Los Angeles	1912	Morgan, Walls & Morgan	280	1020
Title Guarantee & Trust Bldg.	Los Angeles	1930	J. & D. Parkinson	800	2361
Title Insurance & Trust Company	Los Angeles	1927 – 28	J. & D. Parkinson	1251.5	2010
Tribune Bldg.	Oakland	1923	Edw. T. Foulkes	28	1614
UCLA Auditorium	Westwood	1927	Allison & Allison	850	2079
UCLA Chemistry	Westwood	1928	G. W. Kelham	220	2120
UCLA Education	Westwood	1929	G. W. Kelham	414.5	2242
UCLA Library	Westwood	1929	G. W. Kelham		2080
UCLA Mens Gym	Westwood	1931	G. W. Kelham	72	WU #5
UCLA Womens Gym	Westwood	1931	Allison & Allison	270	T1914
UCLA Physics & Biol. Bldg.	Westwood	1928	Allison & Allison	465	T1357
Union Iron Works	San Francisco	1898	Wm. Patton	NA	312
Union Oil Co.	Los Angeles	1911	Parkinson & Bergstrom	349	939
United Artists Theater	Los Angeles	1927	Walker & Eisen	470	T1192
University Club	San Francisco		Bliss & Faville	NA	816
USC Mudd Hall	Los Angeles	1929	R. Flewelling	3	T1551
USC Student Union	Los Angeles	1927	Parkinson & Parkinson	212	T1239
U.S. Post Office & Courthouse	Sacramento	1932	Starks & Flanders	863	2418
U.S. Post Office & Custom House	San Francisco	1899	NA	NA	448
Van Nuys Bldg.	Los Angeles	1912	Morgan, Walls & Morgan	NA	969
Veteran's Bldg. War Memorial	San Francisco	1931	Arthur Brown, Jr.	1615	2387
Weinstock-Lubin & Co.	Sacramento	1923	Powers & Ahnden	92.5	1674
Yolo County Courthouse	Woodland	1916	W. H. Weeks	589	1254

BIBLIOGRAPHY

In writing this book, the author has relied primarily on two principal sources: the Gladding, McBean magazine *Shapes of Clay* (1924–1929; 1937) and company job order files from the Lincoln plant. Three other sources proved essential: the photographic archive of Gladding, McBean in the California State Library; the company's job order book which lists the name of the job, architect, location, date, and type and amount of terra cotta; and company advertisements in the following California architectural magazines: *The Architect and Engineer, California Arts & Architecture, California Southland* and *Pacific Coast Architect.* Taped interviews by Mary Swisher with longtime or retired Lincoln personnel helped fill in gaps. Additionally, the author found the following to be most helpful:

Allen, Harris. "A Building [Bullocks-Wilshire] Designed for Today," *California Arts & Architecture* (January 1930):20–22.
————. "Recent Theaters Designed by G. Albert Lansburgh, Architect," *The Architect and Engineer* (November 1922):49–69.
————. "San Francisco's New Public Utility Buildings," *Pacific Coast Architect* (December 1925):5–25.
————. "Terra Cotta Versus Terra Firma. The New American Architecture Reaches Toward the Sky," *California Arts and Architecture* (February 1930):33–37.
"Atholl McBean is Dead at 89," *San Francisco Chronicle* (December 16, 1968):42.
"The Bank in the Skyscraper," *The Architect and Engineer* (April 1916):38–53.
Battu, Zoe A. "Ornamental Tile — Its History and Renaissance," *Pacific Coast Architect* (May 1927):49.
Bernhardi, Robert. *The Buildings of Oakland.* Oakland: Forest Hill Press, 1979.
————. *Great Buildings of San Francisco, A Photographic Guide.* New York: Dover Publications, Inc., 1980.
"Bullocks' Wilshire Boulevard Store — Los Angeles," *The Architect and Engineer* (December 1929):45–52.
Cahill, J. S. "The Paramount Theater, Oakland," *The Architect and Engineer* (March 1932):10–27.
————. "The Telephone Building, San Francisco," *The Architect and Engineer* (December 1925):51–80.
California, State of. Department of Parks and Recreation. "Historic Resources Inventory." [Sheets describing various buildings held by Office of Historic Preservation, Sacramento].
"California State Life Insurance Building, Sacramento, California," *Pacific Coast Architect* (October 1924):16–17; 39.
California State Mining Bureau. *The Structural and Industrial Materials of California.* Bulletin No. 38 (January 1906).
Clay Products Manual. Clay Products Institute of California. Los Angeles: 1930.
Cline, William Hamilton. "The New Orpheum Theater Building, Los Angeles," *The Architect and Engineer* (September 1911):34–50.
"Competition for an Office Building and Arcade," *The Architect and Engineer* (February 1923):60–70.

Corbett, Michael R. *Splendid Survivors: San Francisco's Downtown Architectural Heritage.* San Francisco: Calif. Living Books, 1979.
Deon, James S. "Brick Featured in Construction of Auditorium," *Sacramento Bee* (February 21, 1927):23.
Dietrich, Waldemar Fenn. *The Clay Resources and the Ceramic Industry of California.* San Francisco: State of California, Division of Mines and Mining. Bulletin No. 99 (January 1928)
Dudley, Mimi and Norman. "Terra Cotta: An Architectural Walking Tour [of Los Angeles]," Los Angeles: Los Angeles Conservancy, 1988.
Ferriday, Virginia Guest. *Last of the Handmade Buildings: Glazed Terra Cotta in Downtown Portland.* Portland: Mark Publishing Company, 1984.
Fitzsimmons, H. L. "Terra Cotta in Building Construction," *The Architect and Engineer* (November 1914):95–99.
"Fort Moore Pioneer Memorial," *Architectural Ceramics* (September 1958):5–12.
Gebhard, David. *The Richfield Building 1928–1968* [Los Angeles: Atlantic-Richfield Company] n.d.
Gebhard, David, and Robert Winter. *A Guide to Architecture in Los Angeles & Southern California.* Salt Lake City: Peregrine Smith Books, 1985.
Gebhard, David, Eric Sandweiss, and Robert Winter. *The Guide to Architecture in San Francisco and Northern California.* Salt Lake City: Peregrine Smith Books, 1985.
Geer, Walter. *The Story of Terra Cotta.* New York: Tobias A. Wright, 1920.
Gladding, McBean and Company. *Catalog Nos. 18, 22, 30, 45 & 50.* San Francisco. Los Angeles. Lincoln.
————. *Ceramic Veneer. The Modern Terra Cotta Facing For Western Construction.* San Francisco: 1936.
————. *Kilnews.* First Anniversary Number (April 6, 1939).
————. *Latin Tiles.* San Francisco: 1923.
————. *Lincoln Plant Centennial 1875–1975* Lincoln: 1975.
————. *Serving the World from Lincoln, Calif. Since 1875.* Lincoln: 1986.
————. *Stock Terra-Cotta.* Los Angeles: 1927.
————. *Gladding, McBean's History 1875–1937: Supervisor's Policy Manual.* San Francisco: 1937.
"Gladding, McBean & Co. Serves Industry and Homes," *The Argonaut* (May 30, 1952):38–39; 43.
Gleye, Paul. *The Architecture of Los Angeles.* Los Angeles: Rosebud Books: 1981.
Hales, George P. *Los Angeles City Hall.* Los Angeles: Board of Public Works of the City of Los Angeles, California. 1928.
————. "The Los Angeles City Hall." *Pacific Coast Architect* (May 1928):13–15; 42–43.
Hamilton, Frederick. "The New Office Building of the Pacific Gas and Electric Company, San Francisco," *The Architect and Engineer* (July 1925):50–56.
————. "Recent Work of Leonard F. Sparks & Co., Sacramento," *The Architect and Engineer* (October 1925):50–75.
Henry, Margaret. "Bay Area Brick and Terra Cotta," in *Festschrift: A Collection of Essays on Architectural History.* Northern Pacific Coast Chapter, Society of Architectural Historians. Salem, Oregon: 1978.
Hopkins, Ernest. "Mudhole Furnishes S.F. Tall Buildings," *San Francisco Examiner* (July 14, 15, 16, 1926).
"Hotel Senator, Sacramento, California," *Pacific Coast Architect* (October 1924):5–9; 11.
Howe, Samuel. "Polychrome Terra Cotta," *The Architect and Engineer* (September 1912):58–65.

Hoye, Daniel. *Art Deco Los Angeles*. Los Angeles: Los Angeles Conservancy, 1988.

Impressions of Imagination: Terra-Cotta Seattle. Seattle: Allied Arts of Seattle Inc. 1986.

"Iron Stone and Terra Cotta Pipe, etc. for all Purposes," *Mining and Scientific Press* (September 22, 1883):182.

Jennings, Frederick. "Recent Hotel Architecture in California," *The Architect and Engineer* (January 1925):56–77.

———. "The Los Angeles City Hall," *The Architect and Engineer* (May 1928):33–39.

Jones, Frederick. W. "The John Breuner Building, Oakland, California," *The Architect and Engineer* (January 1932):16–27.

———. "The Russ Building, San Francisco," *The Architect and Engineer* (September 1927):42–60; 75–89.

Josselyn, Winsor. "Jo Mora, Interpreter of the West," *California Arts & Architecture* (February 1931):39–41; 62.

King, Harry Lee. "A History of Architectural Terra-Cotta," *The Architect and Engineer* (February 1914):84–93.

Knecht, Gary. "Early Uses of Architectural Terra Cotta in the San Francisco Bay Area," Unpublished student paper, University of California, Berkeley, 1980.

Kurutz, K. D. "Molding the Architectural Landscape: Gladding, McBean and Company," *American Ceramics* vol. 4, no. 3 (1985): 24–29.

Lansburgh, G. Albert. "An Architect's Tribute to Domingo Mora," *The Architect and Engineer* (September 1911):51–52.

Lardner, W. B. and M. J. Brock. *History of Placer and Nevada Counties California*. Los Angeles: Historic Record Company: 1924.

Lincoln Arts and Culture Foundation. *Lincoln, California: The Pottery*. Lincoln Arts and Culture Foundation. Lincoln: 1988.

Lincoln News Messenger, "1875–Gladding, McBean . . . Interpace–1975" *Supplement to the News Messenger & Wheatland News*. (May 29, 1975).

Logan, Jerry. *Tales of Western Placer County*. 2 vols. Lincoln: 1985.

Meighan, Charles W. "The Pacific Gas and Electric Co. Building," *Pacific Coast Architect* (December 1925):28–31.

Meyenberg, F. P. "Architectural Terra Cotta as Compared with Stone," *The California Architect and Building News* (July 1891):12.

"The Mills Building." *San Francisco Chronicle* (October 15, 1890).

"Modern Design for Los Angeles Commercial Building [Eastern Outfitting Company]," *Architect and Engineer* (June 1931): 27–29

"The New Hearst Building, San Francisco, Cal.," *The American Architect and Building News* (January 18, 1908):19–21.

"The New Paramount Theater Oakland, California," *California Arts & Architecture* (March 1932):14; 31–33.

"The New San Francisco Pacific Telephone and Telegraph Company Building," *Pacific Coast Architect* (Sept.1924):23; 25; 27; 34.

Nichols, Charles H. "Engineering Features of the New Hearst Building, San Francisco, Cal.," *The American Architect and Building News* (January 18, 1908):21–23.

Olmstead, Roger. *Here Today: San Francisco's Architectural Heritage*. San Francisco: Chronicle Books: 1968.

Pahl, Nikki, Mary Swisher, and Genevieve Troka. *Camera Craft: Commercial Photography of the Sacramento Valley, 1900–1945*. Sacramento: City of Sacramento, Museum and History Division, 1982.

"Peter McGill McBean: Co-Founder, The Gladding, McBean, and Company." *The Bulletin of the American Ceramic Society* (July 1937):314–315.

Piper, John S. "Local Listed Stocks: Gladding, McBean & Co.," *San Francisco Chronicle* (December 24, 1936):14.

Polk, Willis. "The Chronology of an Office Building [Hobart Building]," *The Pacific Coast Architect* (November 1914):178–182; 205.

"Portals of Progress." [The Weinstock-Lubin Building]. *Sacramento Bee* (May 31, 1924):W4.

Pratt, Harry Noyes. "Haig Patigian: California's Noted Sculptor," *Overland Monthly and Out West Magazine* (August 1923):11.

Prosser, Richard. "The Terra-Cotta in the New Telephone Building," *Pacific Coast Architect* (December 1925):61.

Putnam, Edward H. "Architectural Terra Cotta: Its Physical and Structural Properties," *The Brickbuilder* (February 1911):29–33.

Regnery, Dorothy F. "The Capitol Extension Group," *California State Library Foundation Bulletin* (July 1984):1–13; 17.

Rindge, Ronald L., et. al. *Ceramic Art of the Malibu Potteries 1926–1932*. Malibu: Malibu Lagoon Museum: 1988.

Riter, Bradely. "Capital's Magnificent Post Office Is Opened," *Sacramento Bee* (November 4, 1933):12.

Rosenhouse, Leo. "The Pipe Makers of Lincoln," *Westways* (November 1960):26–27.

Speir, Oswald. "Architectural Terra Cotta," *The Architect and Engineer* (October 1915):77–83.

———. "The Development of Architectural Terra Cotta on the Pacific Coast, *The Architect and Engineer* (September 1912): 47–57.

Stanton, J. E. *By Middle Seas: Photographic Studies Reflecting the Architectural Motives of Various Cities on the Mediterranean*. Los Angeles: Gladding, McBean and Co.: 1927.

Stratton, Michael. "The Terracotta Industry: its Distribution, Manufacturing Processes and Products," *Industrial Archaeology Review* (Spring 1986):194–214.

Tempko, Allan. "Oakland May Lose Priceless SP Depot," *San Francisco Chronicle* (January 2, 1989):A4.

"Ten Story Office Building for Fresno Power Company," *The Architect and Engineer* (February 1923):90–91.

"Terra Cotta in Architecture," *The California Architect and Building News* (November 1884):200.

"Terra Cotta: Past to Present," *Architectural Record* (January 1987):110–113.

"Terra Cotta vs. Stone Trimmings," *The California Architect and Building News* (October 1884):189; 201–202.

Tomaschke, F. L. "The New Central Bank Building, Oakland," *The Architect and Engineer* (September 1926): frontispiece: 43–50.

Tucker, W. Burling and Clarence A. Waring. *Mines and Mineral Resources of the Counties of El Dorado, Placer, Sacramento, Yuba*. San Francisco: State of California, California State Mining Bureau, 1917.

Tunick, Susan. *Field Guide to Apartment Building Architecture*. New York: Friends of Terra Cotta: 1986.

Wade, William. "The Architecture of Small Cities," *The Architect and Engineer* (June 1920):4–75.

Weber, Dickinson. *Early Tall Buildings. A Sentimental Sketchbook Collection*. Concord: Sandscape Press: 1988.

Wilson, Mark A. *Living Legacy: Historic Architecture of the East Bay*. San Francisco: Lexikos Press: 1987.

Woodbridge, Sally B. *California Architecture: Historic American Building Survey*. San Francisco: Chronicle Books: 1988.

"The Work of Alfred F. Rosenheim, Architect," *The Architect and Engineer* (March 1907):35–49.

"The Work of John Parkinson and Edwin Bergstrom," *The Architect and Engineer* (September 1910):34–63.

INDEX

MEMBERS OF THE NATIONAL TERRA COTTA SOCIETY, 1922

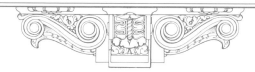

American Terra Cotta & Ceramic Co.
Chicago, IL

Atlanta Terra Cotta Co.
Altanta, GA

Atlantic Terra Cotta Co.
New York, NY

Brick, Terra Cotta & Tile Co.
Corning, NY

N. Clark & Sons
San Francisco, CA

Conkling-Armstrong Terra Cotta Co.
Philadelphia, PA

Denny-Renton Clay & Coal Co.
Seattle, WA

The Denver Terra Cotta Co.
Denver, CO

Federal Terra Cotta Co.
New York, NY

Gladding, McBean & Co.
San Francisco, CA

Indianapolis Terra Cotta Co.
Indianapolis, IN

Kansas City Terra Cotta & Faience Co.
Kansas City, MO

O. W. Ketcham
Philadelphia, PA

Livermore Fire Brick Works
San Francisco, CA

Los Angeles Pressed Brick Co.
Los Angeles, CA

Midland Terra Cotta Co.
Chicago, IL

New Jersey Terra Cotta Co.
New York, NY

New York Architectural Terra Cotta Co.
New York, NY

Northern Clay Co.
Auburn, WA

The Northwestern Terra Cotta Co.
Chicago, IL

St. Louis Terra Cotta Co.
St. Louis, MO

South Amboy Terra Cotta Co.
New York, NY

Tropico Potteries, Inc.
Glendale, CA

Washington Brick, Lime & Sewer Pipe Co.
Spokane, WA

Western Terra Cotta Co.
Kansas City, MO

Winkle Terra Cotta Co.
St. Louis, MO